INDUSTRIAL STRATEGY PROJECT

D1353539

# *Counting the social costs*

## Electricity and externalities in South Africa

CLIVE VAN HOREN

**1996**
**Élan Press and UCT Press**

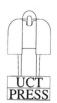

UCT PRESS  *Élan Press*

Published by Élan Press,
EDRC
University of Cape Town
Private Bag
7700 Rondebosch
and
UCT Press
University of Cape Town
Private Bag
7700 Rondebosch

First published 1996

ISBN 0 7992 1743 3

DTP conversion and design: Tim James for EDRC

Printed by UDMS, Observatory

# Contents

# List of tables

# List of figures

# Preface and acknowledgements

This book is the product of a research project undertaken within the 'Labour, Industry and Environment' programme of the Industrial Strategy Project (ISP) over a few months during 1995. The ISP is a Cosatu-linked programme of research, and has produced a number of in-depth studies of South Africa's industrial sector beginning in 1992. Given the importance of the energy sector in the country's economy, coupled with the environmental impacts which are related to the sector, the subject of this book is a logical extension of the ISP's previous work.

Although the subject of externalities is relatively new in the South African policy arena, it has been on international policy agendas for two decades or more. As the policy debates unfold in this country, 'externalities' are appearing more frequently on policy agendas. This book is by no means the final word on the subject - the time and resources available for its preparation did not permit anything more than a first attempt at quantifying external costs. Consequently, the decision to publish it was based not on a presumption that its analysis is complete or definitive, but on the desire to insert the issues, relatively quickly, into the public domain, thereby raising their profile in the South African policy discourse. If the book succeeds in catalysing further work on the subject, then it will have partly achieved its purpose.

Numerous people assisted in this project, particularly in the early stages when information was being gathered, both from South Africa and beyond, many via electronic mail; it is not possible to mention all of these people individually, but their assistance is gratefully acknowledged. I would like, however, to single out for their help and advice, Lael Bethlehem as coordinator of the ISP's 'Labour, industry and environment' programme; Gina Roos, Catherine Fedorsky, Greg Tosen, Clive Turner and several other Eskom staff who were very helpful in supplying technical and other data; David White, Bill Dougherty and Steve Bernow of the Tellus Institute, Boston, and the New York State Electric Energy Research Corporation (respectively, developers and owners of the computer model used in the study); and Mike Holland of ETSU, UK, who offered useful advice on the basis of his experience of a major European externalities study.

In addition, thanks are due to the sponsors of the study, the Friedrich Ebert Stiftung of Germany, who have given considerable support to this and other ISP projects, thereby furthering the development of industrial policy in a democratic South Africa.

The book was laid out and illustrated by my colleague Tim James at the Energy & Development Research Centre, in his usual professional manner.

Finally, this study was undertaken during a time of some work and health stresses for myself and people close to me, and so I wish to dedicate this book to Michelle, who at one stage went so far as to refer to herself as an 'externality' in my life.

*Clive van Horen*
*Cape Town*

# Foreword

South Africa's electricity generator, Eskom, has committed itself to producing the cheapest electricity in the world. It has made considerable progress towards achieving this objective. In consequence, the cost of electricity significantly influences the composition of investment and, hence, the structure of South African industry. However, energy-intensive industrial development embodies complex outcomes for South Africa. From an industrial policy viewpoint, the association of energy intensity with extremely high levels of capital intensity – and this in a society characterised by mass unemployment – is most striking.

In this context then, the notion that society is *subsidising* the cost of this key input demands urgent examination. This book investigates the charge that South Africa's electricity price is artificially low because inadequate attention has been paid to the environmental and associated health costs of its generation. Failure to reflect the environmental and health costs or electricity generation in its price, effectively constitutes a subsidy, a subsidy frequently borne by the poorest members of society and by future generations.

The existence of a significant subsidy would, at the very least, place a question mark against the sustainability of our energy-intensive growth path, not least because of growing global concern with the environmental performance of our electricity industry. In 1995 the Worldwatch Institute reported that South Africa was the world's third-largest producer per capita of greenhouse gases and called for the imposition of carbon taxes to discourage these emissions. Whilst the policy debate around climate change is complex and as yet unresolved both in South Africa and internationally, it appears likely that international and domestic concern will be a growing source of upward pressure on South Africa's electricity price.

In order to develop a coherent industrial policy, South African industrial policy makers must ask two related questions. What are the real costs of pursuing a cheap electricity strategy, and are our low electricity prices sustainable? The Industrial Strategy Project has commissioned this study to assist in answering these vital questions.

Using an internationally tested methodology Clive van Horen traces the social, human and environmental costs of electricity generation and provides a series of estimates of their price effects. The study shows that South Africa has key advantages in producing electricity, including large and accessible coal reserves and a sophisticated, technologically advanced industry. However, van

Horen's study also identifies important environmental impacts associated with the industry. These environmental externalities impose costs on society that are not reflected in the electricity price. This evidence suggests that more attention must be given to improving the industry's environmental performance. This will necessitate sometimes costly investments in technology and management.

In recent years the electricity industry has become increasingly aware of its environmental responsibilities. This is, in small part, evidenced by Eskom's cooperative approach to this study. The purpose of this book is to boost efforts to improve the environmental performance of the industry by showing that the costs of inaction may be greater than the costs of timely intervention. This study is offered as an input into an important debate, as a resource for electricity managers, policymakers, and others concerned with industrial, energy and environmental policy.

This study is part of the second phase of the Industrial Strategy Project. The first phase of the ISP culminated in the publication by UCT Press of 13 sectoral reports and a synthesis volume entitled *Improving Manufacturing Performance in South Africa*. The second phase addresses four themes emerging from the earlier study. These are studies of industrial agglomeration, firm level innovation, work organisation, and the environmental impact of industrial development. This paper is part of the latter study, a full report of which will be published later this year. The ISP was originally conceived as a policy advisory group for the Congress of South African Trade Unions and the ANC. It has retained strong links with both and, obviously, with the new government.

The second phase of the Industrial Strategy Project is funded by the Friedrich Ebert Stiftung of Germany, the Hummanistisch Instituut Voor Ontwikkelingsameerking of the Netherlands, the International Development Research Centre of Canada, and the Olaf Palme International Centre of Sweden. As in the first phase, our funders have provided advice, encouragement and invaluable international input in addition to their generous financial support.

**Lael Bethlehem**
*Coordinator, Industry and the Environment, Industrial Strategy Project*

**David Lewis**
*Director, Industrial Strategy Project*

# Introduction

The electricity sector plays a central role in South Africa's economy – as the supplier of a key input to the industrial, mining and commercial sectors, as an employer, and as a service provider for households. This role is likely to increase in the foreseeable future as the country's reconstruction and development objectives translate into greater economic output and improved service levels for previously-unelectrified households. At the same time, uncertainty exists about the extent to which South Africa's electricity sector is responsible for adverse environmental impacts which are unaccounted or under-accounted for in the current regulatory and pricing regimes. The present project has been initiated as part of the ongoing work of the Industrial Strategy Project, with a view to assessing the significance of the environmental costs of bulk electricity supply.

This chapter provides a brief overview of South Africa's electricity supply industry (ESI) and specifically of the electricity generation sector. It also describes the objective of the present project. In the next chapter, the theory of externalities as described in the economics literature is reviewed and summarised. Chapter Three reviews the major international attempts to account for external costs in the electricity sector, in terms of both the quantitative results produced by those exercises, and their methodological approaches. In Chapter Four, the main externalities in South Africa's electricity sector are identified, with a focus on the coal-based subsector but including aspects related to the nuclear-based electricity industry. In Chapter Five, economic valuations of key externalities are made, and these results are compared to current price levels. In the final chapter, some policy implications of the analysis are briefly addressed.

## An overview of South Africa's electricity supply industry

South Africa's ESI comprises three main subsectors, corresponding to their functional activities: the *generation* of electricity, its *transmission* from power stations through a high-voltage national network and, finally, the *distribution* of electricity from the transmission network to consumers. Whilst the focus of this project is on the generation sector, it is worth briefly describing the transmission and distribution sectors.

The transmission sector is owned and operated almost exclusively by Eskom, with the exception of a small amount of high-voltage transmission undertaken by distributors. At the end of 1994 Eskom's main transmission network, operating at a voltage of 132 kV and above, consisted of a total of about 25 000 kilometres of lines; including its low and medium voltage lines, its total network consisted of about 239 000 kilometres of lines (Eskom 1995a: 57). The operation and management of the national transmission system is entirely under Eskom's control and is the responsibility of the Executive Director: Transmission. Since Eskom operates as a vertically integrated utility, with no separate public reporting for its divisions, there is little public data about the financial flows associated with the transmission sector.

*Distribution*
The distribution sector of the ESI is highly fragmented and is currently undergoing fairly significant re-organisation. Until the early 1990s, the distribution industry was dominated by local authority distributors which purchased electricity in bulk from Eskom and sold it to their commercial, industrial and domestic consumers. Although Eskom had many industrial and domestic consumers to whom it supplied electricity directly, it was not until 1991 that the annual growth rate in its number of customers exceeded 10%. Table 1.1 shows the increase in the number of Eskom's direct customers over the period 1970 to 1994 for three categories of consumers: domestic (mainly households), non-domestic, and bulk consumer. 'Bulk' consumers comprise mainly local authority electricity distributors.

|       | *Domestic* | *Non-domestic* | *Bulk* | *Total* |
|-------|-----------|---------------|--------|---------|
| 1970  | 98 155    | 16 630        | 265    | 115 050 |
| 1980  | 109 558   | 69 865        | 419    | 179 842 |
| 1990  | 111 709   | 129 872       | 673    | 242 254 |
| 1991  | 142 759   | 134 278       | 704    | 277 741 |
| 1992  | 397 562   | 143 284       | 718    | 541 564 |
| 1993  | 715 219   | 156 241       | 742    | 872 202 |
| 1994  | 1 053 725 | 152 624       | 704    | 1 207 053 |

**Table 1.1**  Number of Eskom's customers from 1970 to 1994
*(Eskom 1994: 23, 1995a: 58)*

It is evident from the table that the number of Eskom's customers grew considerably from 1992 onwards, and this reflects two important structural changes in the ESI during this period. Firstly, Eskom launched its electrification programme at the end of 1990 and connected an additional 685 000 homes from 1991 to 1994 (Van Horen 1995). Its stated goal is to electrify 1.75 million homes during the period 1994 to 1999, or 70% of the target contained in the Reconstruction and Development Programme – 2.5 million homes (ANC 1994: 33). Secondly, Eskom transferred large numbers of customers onto its accounts following the collapse of service provision in many historically-black local authorities and in some of the former homeland areas. The effect was to widen Eskom's focus from its traditional concern with bulk generation and transmission of electricity, with only a relatively small distribution function, to include the distribution and marketing of electricity to consumers.

At the same time, significant changes have been taking place among local authority (LA) electricity distributors. Historically, this sector has been highly fragmented along racial lines, with over 400 LA distributors around 1990 (Dingley 1992: 21). Recent trends include the consolidation of the jurisdictions of formerly racially-separate LAs and the re-issuing of licences to these consolidated authorities. Through this process, coupled with the take-over of supply areas by Eskom, the number of distributors has decreased considerably since the early 1990s.

A key stakeholder in the ESI, especially with respect to the electrification programme, is the National Electricity Regulator (NER) which was established in early 1995 on the recommendation of the National Electrification Forum.[1] Whilst the principal concern of the NER is presently with matters related to the electrification programme, such as issuing licences to distributors and overseeing the rationalisation of the distribution industry, its role is unlikely to be permanently limited to electrification issues. In fact, in many countries with large electricity supply industries, electricity regulatory agencies have taken on a critical role in a range of governance issues, including the environmental performance of the industry. It might be expected, therefore, that the NER will widen its scope to include such issues at some point in the future, once the more urgent priorities around restructuring of the ESI have been resolved.

---

1    The National Electrification Forum (NELF) was a body representing all key stakeholders in the electricity industry, established in 1993 to formulate policies for an accelerated electrification programme for South Africa. It was disbanded in early 1995, having reached agreement on some issues; but since it could make decisions only by consensus, it was unable to resolve several important policy questions.

*Generation*

Eskom is the key player in the electricity generation sector: in 1994 it generated 96% of all electricity in South Africa, with the balance being produced by some local authorities with their own power stations (such as Johannesburg, Port Elizabeth and Cape Town) and by private concerns producing electricity for their own consumption (Eskom 1995a: 54). Most of the municipal power stations are used as a backup to the Eskom supply, and have not been fully operational for some time, with the exception of those in Johannesburg, which have ready access to cheap coal (Steyn 1994: 7).[2] Given the dominance of Eskom in the electricity generation sector, therefore, the remainder of this report focuses on its own power stations. This is not to imply, however, that the environmental impacts of local authorities' power stations are less significant than those of Eskom's power stations in relative terms – if anything, the opposite is true, given that LA stations are generally older, less efficient and located in more densely populated areas – but their size in relation to Eskom's capacity does not warrant further attention here.

As at the end of 1994 Eskom had 19 power stations in commission, with a total nominal capacity of 37 840 MW (Eskom 1995a: 56). A breakdown of this capacity by fuel source is given in Table 1.2.

|  | No. of stations | Location | Nominal capacity (MW) | % of total |
|---|---|---|---|---|
| Coal-fired | 12 | Mpumalanga (10), Free State, Northern Province | 33 568 | 88.7 |
| Nuclear | 1 | Western Cape | 1 930 | 5.1 |
| Gas turbine | 2 | Western Cape, Eastern Cape | 342 | 0.9 |
| Hydroelectric | 2 | Free State | 600 | 1.6 |
| Pumped storage | 2 | KwaZulu-Natal, Western Cape | 1 400 | 3.7 |
| Total | 19 |  | 37 840 | 100.0 |

**Table 1.2**  Breakdown of Eskom's generation capacity as at
31 December 1994
*(Eskom 1995a: 56)*

---

2    The Cape Town electricity department recommissioned its Athlone Power station in 1995 for the purpose of meeting demand during peak periods.

It is evident from the table that 95% of total electricity capacity is based on non-renewable resources: primarily coal, but including also nuclear and small amounts of gas. The coal and nuclear power stations provide the bulk of the base electricity load, while the pumped storage schemes and gas turbines are used primarily to meet electricity demand at the peak and in cases of emergency. Pumped storage schemes are net consumers of electricity, which is used during off-peak hours to pump water up to storage reservoirs, and then allowed to run down during peak hours when electricity demand is especially high.

Of the total capacity of 37 840 MW, some 4 531 MW or 12% was mothballed as at the end of 1994 (Eskom 1995a: 56), because of the excess capacity on Eskom system – these were generally the older and less efficient stations. Peak demand in 1994 was 24 798 MW (Eskom 1995a: 2), reflecting the large amount of excess capacity, even with the standard reserve margins commonly employed by utilities for safety reasons. In 1995, however, the peak demand on the system came much closer to supply capacity. Eskom operated nine of its coal power stations during 1994; their location and that of Koeberg nuclear power station is shown in Figure 1.1.

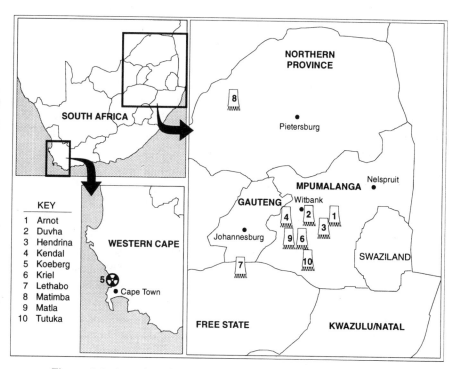

**Figure 1.1** Location of Eskom's operational coal and nuclear power stations, 1994

The dominance of coal in the actual *production* of electricity is even more significant. Table 1.3 shows the total number of units of electricity generated by each of the main supply sources for the period 1990 to 1994.

| | 1994 | | 1993 | | 1992 | | 1991 | |
|---|---|---|---|---|---|---|---|---|
| | GWh | % | GWh | % | GWh | % | GWh | % |
| Coal-fired | 148 003 | 92.3 | 145 514 | 94.3 | 136 830 | 92.3 | 135 743 | 91.3 |
| Nuclear | 9 697 | 6.0 | 7 255 | 4.7 | 9 288 | 6.3 | 9 144 | 6.2 |
| Gas turbine | 2 | 0.0 | 0 | 0.0 | 4 | 0.0 | 0 | 0.0 |
| Hydroelectric | 1 074 | 0.7 | 146 | 0.1 | 752 | 0.5 | 1 980 | 1.3 |
| Pumped storage | 1 517 | 1.0 | 1 345 | 0.9 | 1 333 | 0.9 | 1 804 | 1.2 |
| Total | 160 293 | 100.0 | 154 260 | 100.0 | 148 207 | 100.0 | 148 671 | 100.0 |

**Table 1.3** Breakdown of Eskom's electricity generated
for the period 1991 to 1994
*(Eskom 1995a: 54-55)*

Comparing the data in Tables 1.2 and 1.3, it is evident that coal generated 92% of all electricity in 1994, even though coal-fired power stations constituted a somewhat lower percentage of total capacity (89%) – this reflects the high level of utilisation of coal plants which are used for base-load. The Koeberg nuclear power station has supplied a relatively constant 5% to 6% of Eskom's electricity. Whilst the contribution of the two pumped storage schemes has been relatively constant at around only 1%, the amount of electricity generated by the hydroelectric schemes dropped considerably in 1992 and 1993 – this was due to the drought which affected the flow rate of the Orange River. It is clear, therefore, that the most significant component of the generation sector, in terms of electricity output, is the *coal-based* sector. The primary focus of this report is therefore on that part of the industry. This is appropriate, given that coal-based electricity is generally associated with significant externalities, and these have been studied widely in other countries. Nuclear power, although contributing less than 10% of South Africa's electricity, has also been analysed fairly extensively internationally on the basis of its actual and potential external costs, and some consideration will be given to the impacts of the local nuclear industry.

# Eskom in an international context

Eskom is one of the largest electricity utilities in the world, when compared either on the basis of generation capacity, or on the basis of actual units of electricity produced. Table 1.4 gives the ten largest utilities in the world and shows that Eskom ranks in the top five. Eskom is one of only two utilities from non-OECD countries in the top ten, and South Africa the country with the lowest per capita GDP (World Bank 1993). Eskom is therefore an unusually strong utility amongst developing countries.

| Utility | Country | Annual sales (GWh) | Ranking by sales | Nominal capacity (MW) | Ranking by capacity |
|---|---|---|---|---|---|
| EDF | France | 372 400 | 1 | 98 100 | 1 |
| TEPCO | Japan | 231 665 | 2 | 49 492 | 3 |
| ENEL | Italy | 197 451 | 3 | 50 888 | 2 |
| Hydro-Quebec | Canada | 152 099 | 4 | 29 131 | 7 |
| Eskom | S Africa | 143 800 | 5 | 39 746 | 4 |
| Ontario Hydro | Canada | 127 777 | 6 | 33 793 | 6 |
| Korea Electric Power Co | S Korea | 127 734 | 7 | 27 654 | 8 |
| Kansai Electric Power Co | Japan | 123 300 | 8 | 35 035 | 5 |
| RWE | Germany | 121 504 | 9 | 25 777 | 9 |
| TVA | USA | 118 560 | 10 | 25 622 | 10 |

**Note**
All data as at 31 December 1993, except for TEPCO (31 March 1994), ENEL (31 December 1992), RWE (30 June 1993) and TVA (30 September 1993). The difference between Eskom's sales in this table (143 800 GWh) and its production in Table 1.3 (154 260 GWh) is due mainly to transmission losses and to electricity which is consumed by its own power stations (mostly pumped storage stations

**Table 1.4** The largest electricity utilities in the world, 1993
(Eskom 1995a: 59)

Another important point of comparison between Eskom and international electricity utilities is their relative price levels. Eskom is amongst the cheapest producers of electricity in the world;[3] at the end of 1993, its industrial electricity

---

3    This comparison excludes utilities whose tariffs are too low to recover their costs.

tariffs were the lowest of a basket of industrialised countries: Japan (whose average price was over three times higher than Eskom's), Germany, the United Kingdom, the United States, France, Canada, New Zealand and Sweden (Eskom 1995a: 9). This comparison is all the more striking when the resource bases of some of those countries are taken into account: in particular, several of the listed countries are predominantly hydro-electricity based – this is generally regarded as one of the cheapest sources of electricity. The question therefore arises: why is South Africa's electricity so cheap in relative terms?

## Trends in Eskom's electricity prices

A notable development in relation to Eskom's electricity prices is its ongoing commitment to reduce the real price of electricity on the back of internal efficiency gains. Eskom announced its 'price compact' in 1991, in terms of which it undertook to decrease the real price of electricity by 20% over the five-year period 1992-1996. This followed a 14% reduction in real price which had already been achieved from 1987 to 1991 (Eskom 1992: 5). In 1994, it made a further commitment, in terms of its 'RDP commitments' to reduce the real price by 15% over the period 1995-2000 (1995a: 9). Until 1994, all of these targets had been met, which means that 1994 prices were approximately 76% of 1987 levels in real terms. There is little reason to believe that the utility will not meet its latest commitment and, if this is the case, the average electricity price in 2000 will be approximately 60%, in real terms, of the 1987 price level – a dramatic decrease by any standards.

Eskom suggests that these price reductions will be achieved through ongoing productivity improvements, reduced operating expenditure and cost containment. This commitment is linked to the goal of becoming 'the world's lowest-cost producer of electricity' (1992: 3). It is evident that other factors underlie the decrease in electricity prices, notably the reduction in the number of employees, from 66 000 in 1985 to 40 000 in 1994 (1992: 55). In addition, its reduced exposure to finance charges has contributed significantly to its financial health, with the debt: equity ratio having declined from 3.0: 1 in 1985, to its 1994 level of 1.7: 1 (1992: 10). The utility's stated intention is to reduce this ratio to parity by 1998; this is possible, given that its levels of capital expenditure have declined considerably in real terms since the mid-1980s because of the situation of over-capacity in which Eskom found itself (Van Horen 1995). It is in this context that the question again arises, as to whether South Africa's electricity prices, declining in real terms, adequately reflect environmental costs.

With a strong downward trend in electricity prices, it is pertinent also to consider what the implications of this are for the country's overall economic development path. Low energy prices, especially if they are amongst the lowest in the world, provide a very strong signal to energy consumers and to potential investors. All other things equal, low prices are likely to encourage a heavily energy- and resource-intensive growth path which, once taken, is likely to be difficult to re-direct. Most of the world's wealthiest nations, on the other hand, have increasingly decoupled economic output from energy input; indeed, electricity prices in countries such as Japan and Germany are amongst the world's highest. Although there are obviously many other factors influencing the performance of any economy, it is not implausible that higher electricity prices may have played a key role in encouraging their economies to shift away from a resource-intensive base to a higher value-added base, and that this shift has had positive implications for their economic performance in the long term. If this is so, then it would be important to consider the South African case: whether, in fact, the goal of achieving the world's lowest electricity prices could be detrimental to long-term economic performance. The internalisation of environmental costs obviously impacts upon general electricity price levels. The issue raised here, however, is a wider question within industrial policy; as it is beyond the scope of the present report, it can only be noted here as an important policy issue.

## Project objective

The aim of this project is to assess the environmental costs incurred in the production of electricity in South Africa, in particular of those 'external' costs which are not accounted for in the price of electricity. The investigation takes as its point of departure the explicit recognition that, on the one hand, cheap and abundant supplies of electricity represent one of South Africa's important comparative advantages and offer significant opportunities for industrial growth, while, on the other hand, there may be significant environmental costs which are not accounted for and which could have serious consequences for current and future environmental, social and economic performance.

This is an important issue as it affects government policy in at least three sectors: firstly, the industrial sector, as a major consumer of electricity; secondly, the energy sector as the producer of electricity; and thirdly, the environmental sector, as the stewards of environmental quality. From the point of view of South Africa's industrial policy, the availability of cheap electricity at low prices is an important comparative advantage on which to base further economic growth. This is evident in large electricity-intensive investments which have already been made, such as the Alusaf aluminium smelter in Richards Bay, and in attempts to solicit new investments. At the opening of the sub-station built to serve Alusaf, Eskom's chairman, Dr John Maree, suggested: 'Cheap power would allow us [Southern African economies] to achieve growth rates not seen before in Africa' (quoted in The Argus, 22 June 1995). Similarly, at an international investment conference in 1994, Dr Louis van Pletsen, then head of the Chief Executive's office, urged: 'access to reliable and internationally competitive electricity should entice investment in electricity intensive industries to South Africa and enable it to potentially become the "electricity valley" of the world, analogous to a "silicon valley" in the USA' (1994: 4).

Electricity-intensive industrial activity may make a significant contribution to economic growth and exports, and lead to a modest increase in permanent employment, but it generally also has significant resource implications, in terms of both inputs of electricity and outputs of waste. For present purposes, the crucial question for industrial policy-makers is whether it is appropriate to invest heavily in electricity-intensive industries, on the basis of electricity's low price, if, in fact, it is cheap only or largely because environmental standards are so low that electricity is effectively subsidised by the environment and society. If the price of electricity is too low, this line of reasoning goes, then industrial consumers and potential investors would be given an inaccurate signal, which could lead to a misallocation of scarce resources.

For the energy sector similar questions arise, but from the supply-side. Energy policy-makers have a responsibility to encourage the efficient, equitable and sustainable use of energy resources, and all of these will be facilitated through realistic pricing of electricity. Finally, environmental policy-makers have a stewardship responsibility for the country's resources and for the quality of the natural and social environments; this requires giving consideration to the management of environmental impacts and, increasingly, the adequate pricing of natural resources.

# 2

# The economic theory of externalities and market failure

There is a large body of economic literature which deals with the theory of externalities and market failure; it is important to understand this theory, because of the complex methodological questions which arise in practical attempts to apply it. This section therefore briefly reviews the theory of externalities and of possible market interventions to address them. It also outlines the main approaches to the valuation of environmental impacts.

## The theory of externalities

A central concept in the economic analysis of environmental impacts is that of an externality. An externality or 'external effect' can be either positive or negative, although policy is most frequently concerned with the latter. It is sometimes defined so broadly as to include most sources of market failure, although in its more contemporary usage it generally refers to a situation where two conditions are met:

- activity by one economic agent causes a change in the utility or welfare of another agent; and

- this change in welfare is not compensated or appropriated (Baumol & Oates 1981: 17; Pearce & Turner 1990: 61).

An externality therefore arises in situations such as where a productive facility causes the emission of pollutants or waste products which, in turn, impact upon human health or other things which have value for humans (such as agricultural crops), where the costs of those impacts are not captured in the market relationship between the producer and its customers, and those who bear the costs are not compensated in any way. It is apparent that this scenario applies to electricity production insofar as it has environmental and health impacts, the costs of which are not accounted for in the utility's costing or pricing regime.

Another way of explaining the idea of externalities is by reference to the divergence between private and social costs (Pearce & Turner 1990: 66). Private costs are those which are borne by the producer of the good: in Eskom's case, these would comprise the costs of the factors of production – coal, enriched uranium, labour, capital and so on. Social costs go further than this and include the full costs of producing or consuming a commodity, and may be borne not only by the producer but also by other groups in society. Thus, in the case of South African electricity, its social cost would include, in addition to the private cost incurred by electricity generators, the costs of, for example, impaired health resulting from air pollution emitted by power stations, of reduced forest productivity caused by acidic deposition and the increased mortality burden on coal miners.

The difference between private and social costs, then, represents the *external cost* or the externality which is borne by society at large. This means that the market-based relationship between the producer and consumer, as reflected in the price, does not reflect external costs since these are borne by other members of society. Invariably, the *distribution* of these costs is such that they are not borne equitably by society as a whole, but fall more heavily on some groups or classes than others.

The principles of external costs are illustrated graphically in Figure 2.1. Any individual producer faces a horizontal marginal revenue curve (MR) equivalent to the price of the commodity, and a marginal private cost curve as shown by MPC. If the producer seeks to maximise its surplus, it will clearly produce at the point where its marginal revenues and costs are equal: point B, that is, at a level of output equal to $Q_1$. With the assumption that it seeks to maximise profits, it makes little sense to deviate to either side of that point.[1] The marginal external cost at any given level of output is given by the vertical difference between the MSC and MPC lines, and so the total external cost at the individual's optimum ($Q_1$) is equal to the triangle ODB.

---

1    To illustrate this, consider any levels output to the left of $Q_1$: there the marginal revenue from increasing the level of output will exceed the marginal (private) cost and so it makes sense to increase production. As soon as output increases beyond $Q_1$, however, marginal cost exceeds marginal revenue and so it makes sense to decrease output until $Q_1$ is reached: hence there is no advantage to be gained from deviating to either side of $Q_1$.

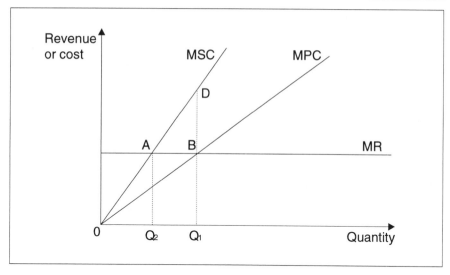

**Figure 2.1** Illustrative marginal revenue (MR), marginal private cost (MPC) and marginal social cost (MSC) curves in a competitive market

Whilst this may be optimal from the individual producer's perspective, it is not ideal for society as a whole. The *socially* optimum level of output will be at a lower point, that is, point A, where the marginal benefit equals the marginal *social* cost, equivalent to a level of output of $Q_2$. At this point, the benefits to society are exactly equal to the costs to society of producing the commodity, and so, if the objective is to maximise *social* welfare – rather than individuals' surpluses – then it does not make sense to deviate to either side of $Q_2$.

It is worth noting that, in terms of this formulation, which is derived from basic microeconomics, the economic optimum will still be associated with *some* level of pollution, the external costs of which are shown by the triangle OAC in the figure. This is an important point of departure in economic analysis, namely that there is an optimal level of pollution, which is often above zero, and that this depends upon the interplay between costs and benefits. In an environmental analysis, by contrast, the optimum level of pollution is usually at or close to zero, corresponding to very low levels of economic activity, and this depends not upon costs and benefits, but upon ecological processes. This highlights the frequently differing approaches of economists and environmentalists in analysing pollution and related issues.

The theory as outlined above therefore demonstrates that externalities constitute an important source of market failure. If the above conceptual representation bears any relation to reality, then it can be expected that the existence of externalities may lead to several outcomes which are less than ideal. Firstly, resources could be allocated inefficiently due to the decision of producers to produce a higher level of output than is economically ideal. Secondly, the burdens of the external costs are seldom spread equitably across society and often fall on social groups which are least able to afford them. Thirdly, a higher rate of productive activity usually translates into more rapid consumption of resources, including non-renewable ones, and this undermines goals of environmental sustainability. Collectively, the effect of externalities is therefore in conflict with goals of economic efficiency, social equity and environmental sustainability – the three pillars upon which 'sustainable development' is based. Where this situation exists, there is thus a clear need for policy interventions to ameliorate the negative effects described.

## The theory of achieving the 'optimal' level of pollution

Left to itself, the market will generally not produce an efficient (or equitable or sustainable) result in situations where externalities exist. The economics literature has also recognised this, and has accordingly analysed a range of options for dealing with external costs. The objective of these options is generally the same: to achieve a level of output which will approximate the socially optimum level. Four categories of response have been suggested in the literature, each of which is described briefly below.

### Laissez-faire or free market bargaining options

The first approach to achieving the optimal level of pollution is perhaps the most theoretical and least practicable in relation to power sector externalities. It entails a *laissez-faire* approach in which the polluter and pollutee(s) are left to bargain with each other over the level of pollution and any associated compensation which may be required. In terms of what is known as the Coase Theorem, it is suggested that if a market-like bargaining process can be established, a socially-optimum level of pollution will result without any direct government involvement (Coase 1960).

While policy-making would be simple (or unnecessary) if the Coase Theorem were true in practice, this is patently not the case. Numerous criticisms have been directed at this theory (Fisher 1981: 184; Pearce & Turner 1990: 73), most notably that it cannot apply in cases where there are large numbers of parties affected by the pollution from any one source (as is the case with power station impacts), let alone where there are many sources of pollution. The 'transaction costs' – the costs of undertaking this bargaining process – would be prohibitively high in reality. Moreover, the theory assumes that all participants in this process would have access to full knowledge about the pollution and its effects, which is also not true in reality. Finally, the bargaining approach envisaged by Coase could entail a 'solution' whereby poor pollutees pay wealthy polluters to reduce pollution – while theoretically efficient, the inequity of such a situation renders it untenable as a practical solution.

It is evident then that, in reality, the *laissez-faire* bargaining option does not occur spontaneously as the Coase Theorem suggests it might, and even if it did it could prove unacceptable; thus some form of intervention is usually required to achieve an acceptable level of pollution.

### Environmental standards and regulations

The second response to pollution which has been extensively analysed in the literature, is the most commonly employed option, namely the use of regulations and standards. These are usually set with reference to health-related criteria and can take a number of forms: limits on the quantity of pollutants which may be emitted by producers, specifications of the technologies to be employed in certain processes, limits on the ambient concentration of pollutants in the atmosphere, and legislation affecting technological choices, inputs and wastes. Environmental standards have both advantages and disadvantages, with the most important positive factor being their relative simplicity and ease of implementation, which probably accounts for their widespread use in practice (Pearce & Turner 1990: 102). In many countries, standards and regulations have been the first pollution control instruments implemented by governments. They are usually considered to be most appropriate in two scenarios: firstly, where the pollutants are so hazardous as to require very strict controls on their use, which can be achieved through direct regulation; secondly, standards are suitable in conditions where markets do not operate freely, and where there is insufficient capacity in governments and regulatory agencies to devise, implement and operate more complex systems of pollution taxes and tradable permits.

In spite of the practical advantages and widespread employment of standards, they have been criticised in the literature on the grounds that they seldom result in economically efficient control outcomes (Pearce & Turner 1990: 102-106), mainly because regulators seldom have adequate information to enable them to set standards at a level which will achieve the 'optimal' level of output ($Q_2$ in Figure 2.1). Another disadvantage of standards is that they require fairly significant resources for their enforcement, and if these resources are not available, the effectiveness of the system is undermined. Generally, polluters would assess the probability of being caught transgressing regulations, together with the severity of the penalty, and then base their production and technology choices on that assessment. Clearly, if penalties are low, or the enforcement function is weak, they face low risks if they pollute. A third disadvantage of standards is that, by themselves, they offer little incentive to producers to innovate and reduce pollution levels below the acceptable limit, even though damage costs may not be insignificant.

## Pollution taxes and subsidies

The third pollution control option centres around the use of pollution taxes (and sometimes subsidies) to correct for external costs not ordinarily reflected in private decision-making (Helm & Pearce 1990: 5). The intellectual work analysing this option was done as far back as 1920, and usually envisages the imposition of a pollution tax or levy to bring the producer's private cost function in line with the social cost function, thereby encouraging the producer to adjust its level of output to the socially desirable level (Pigou 1920). This 'Pigovian tax' underlies the contemporary terminology of the 'polluter pays principle'. Pollution taxes enjoy more favourable reviews in the economics literature because they are held to achieve pollution reductions more efficiently than other options such as standards (Pearce & Turner 1990: 102; Baumol & Oates 1981: 164). This is mainly because pollution taxes provide incentives to reduce pollution levels and leave it up to producers to decide on the least-cost methods of doing so. A second advantage of pollution taxes is that they can deliver social benefits, even in the context of uncertainty and lack of information, as long as the tax brings the polluter's cost function closer to the social cost function.

Another benefit of the pollution tax option is that it can generate revenues for government. The theory suggests very clearly that this should not be seen as a general revenue-raising method for the fiscus, but rather that any revenues should be dedicated to administration of the system and to enhance environmental quality. Thus a cross-subsidy effect could be possible, whereby polluters contribute to improved environmental performance. Whilst this option has found favour in recent years, it must also be noted that it is subject to limitations, one of which is the practical difficulty of estimating the relevant MSC and MPC curves or even their approximate position and shape (Helm & Pearce 1990: 5). More technical issues also arise, such as where there are multiple equilibrium points arising from non-convexities in the cost functions, which could occur, for example, when there are step-changes in pollution due to remedial action or technological change occurring at some level of pollution (Fisher 1981: 176).

## Marketable emissions permits

The fourth and last category of pollution control approaches which is extensively analysed in the literature is the use of marketable emissions permits (MEPs), also called tradable permits. As in the case of environmental standards, the regulatory authorities specify a maximum permissible amount of a particular pollutant which can be emitted, and then issue permits equivalent to that amount. In this case, however, the permits can be traded in a market. This option has a number of theoretical advantages (Pearce & Turner 1990: 111-115). Firstly, MEPs will encourage the attainment of a least-cost solution, since producers with relatively low abatement costs will prefer to reduce their emissions and sell their permits, while those with high abatement costs will prefer to buy permits allowing them to emit pollution, rather than incur high abatement costs. In this way, the theory suggests, pollution control goals are achieved in the least-cost manner. Secondly, MEPs (unlike penalties and taxes) are not denominated in monetary terms and thus do not need to be adjusted for inflation over time. Thirdly, the system is flexible enough to allow the regulator (or even other interested parties) to reduce the permissible level of pollution by buying up permits if this is desired. Finally, the MEP system is intended to accommodate changing conditions through its price mechanism: changes in environmental standards, shock impacts of lumpy investments in capital equipment and uncertainty can all be accounted for through price changes rather than by having to adjust standards or taxes.

Tradable permits have been employed in several countries, most notably the US, where the 1990 amendments to the Clean Air Act established a national cap on sulphur dioxide emissions and an allowance trading system for these emissions (Bernow et al. 1991: 12). Whilst practical experience to-date with these systems is still relatively limited, indications are that the tradable permit approach can be less cost-effective than promised, because of the existence of high transaction costs (Stavins 1995: 9). These costs are associated with creating and managing a market in which prospective buyers and sellers of the permits can meet and trade, and with ensuring that permit holders do not exceed their allowable quotas. Another disadvantage with MEP systems is that, although they achieve pollution control goals at least-cost, (unlike pollution taxes) they do not contain any in-built incentives to innovate and reduce pollution below the specified levels. Finally, where there are other market problems – in addition to the existence of externalities – such as a monopolistic industry structure, opportunities arise for hoarding of permits not on the basis of relative abatement costs, but as a means of maintaining or increasing control over the market. This could have inequitable and inefficient results. Likewise, where trading in permits is 'thin', change will happen very slowly and the least-cost situation may be slow to materialise.

## Environmental valuation methods

Central to the process of internalising external costs is the valuation of those costs in monetary terms. This is a complex and controversial area, with a huge amount of literature taking various positions on the ethics, practicalities and technicalities of environmental valuation (see, for example, Pearce et al. 1989: 51; Cooper 1981: 8; Jacobs 1991: 204). It is not possible to comprehensively review valuation approaches in this report, but in order that subsequent methodological discussions have meaning, the main categories of valuation methods are described briefly.

Cooper (1981: 51) employs a useful distinction to differentiate between two kinds of environmental externalities: first, impacts which reduce economic *outputs* or increase the cost of inputs, in which case damage costs are measured directly by the foregone (net) output; secondly, impacts which affect peoples' *welfare*, apart from the effect on output, and in this case damage cost is usually measured by peoples' willingness to pay to have the impact abated. Valuation of the former category is generally simpler and less controversial because reference can be made directly to a market; thus if acidic deposition causes a decrease in the productivity of commercial forests, then the damage costs can be calculated in terms of foregone output. Valuation of the second category, however, is less simple and a number of methods have been devised. The first three methods described below fall into the second category, while the last two methods are applicable to the first category, namely those which affect economic output or input costs.

### Contingent valuation methods

Contingent valuation methods (CVM) usually involve the use of questionnaires to gauge people's willingness to pay (WTP) for an improved environment, or willingness to accept (WAC) compensation for a worse environment. On the basis of the hypothetical market thus created, an imputed value is derived for the environmental commodity or service in question. The attraction of this option is that it can be used to value any environmental aspect, even if there is no market relationship whatsoever.

CVM approaches have been widely used in North America and Europe as well as some developing countries. Even proponents of CVM, however, acknowledge that it is prone to a number of serious weaknesses, which are usually exacerbated in developing country contexts (Cooper 1981: 76). Many problems exist, but chief amongst these are that CVM simply aggregates valuations derived from study respondents, usually without making any adjustment for unequal income distributions. Clearly, if a poor person places a value of one Rand on something, it has a higher value for that person than a one Rand valuation from a rich person; therefore to derive a social valuation by aggregating all individual valuations is highly problematic. To adjust valuations by some weighting factor to take account of unequal income distributions increases the level of uncertainty further.

## Hedonic pricing methods

This approach derives valuations for environmental components from market transactions in related goods or services, most usually land and property prices, but also wages. The reasoning is that those market prices already embody valuations of their related environmental conditions (for example, noise pollution from a nearby airport). Likewise, it is assumed that wages reflect occupational exposures to health and other risks. Valuations of environmental aspects are then usually derived using statistical methods to isolate the variances in prices attributable to the environmental issue in question. This approach also has numerous problems, especially in contexts where markets do not operate efficiently, since this means that it will be impossible to detect the impact of the selected environmental factors on price levels. This is often the case in developing countries, where housing markets are often informal or non-existent and wages do not adequately reflect occupational hazards.

## Travel cost methods

Travel cost methods derive valuations for environmental resources on the basis of actual expenditure incurred by people travelling to and from such resources. This is most commonly applied to value game reserves and recreation areas. Again, this approach is of little value in many contexts outside of the specific ones in which it has been used and, furthermore, is not easily applicable to externalities in the electricity sector.

## Control cost methods

This approach is sometimes used in the valuation of externalities produced by the power sector, and essentially uses the cost of environmental protection as a surrogate for damage costs. These are relatively easy to assess since control costs are accounted for by utilities, but the logic for their application is not compelling. In general, there is no reason why the costs of preventing or mitigating an externality should bear any relationship to the actual damage costs of the externalities. If anything, control costs should constitute one side of the cost-benefit equation, with the other (benefit) side comprising the avoided damages resulting from the employment of those controls. It is in this context that control costs are an important area for policy-making.

A sub-set of the control cost approach which has been used by some analysts is the 'regulator's revealed preference' approach, which will be discussed in more detail later in this report.

## Opportunity cost methods

The final method for deriving environmental valuations focuses on opportunity costs. In brief, these valuation methods focus on the actual costs or foregone income which can be attributed to a given impact. For instance, air pollution emissions can be valued at the total of the expenditure on medical care, travel costs for visits to doctors and hospitals and foregone income due to absence from work. This valuation approach enjoys the advantage of being the most closely related to real-world economic transactions, although it may not fully reflect individuals' or society's valuation of impacts. This method is described in more detail in Chapter Five.

## Conclusion

It should already be apparent from this review of the theory underpinning externalities and their internalisation that, while the theory of externalities and their internalisation is fairly straightforward, the practice is much more complex. The following chapter reviews international attempts to internalise external costs, both in terms of the methodologies adopted and the valuations derived. Discussion henceforth is thus specifically concerned with externalities generated by the electricity industry.

# 3

# *International attempts to account for externalities*

There have been several major initiatives in the past decade to account for external costs arising in the power sectors of developed countries. In addition to these major externality studies, there have also been numerous smaller studies in which external costs have been estimated for specific classes of environmental impacts. Many of these micro studies have been utilised in the valuation components of the larger externality studies. This section reviews the major externality projects, taking account of the smaller-scale studies only to the extent that their results have been incorporated into the former.

Externalities studies employ widely differing methodologies, which account in large measure for the different numerical valuations they yield (Lee 1995: 2). Methodological approaches can be usefully categorised as being either 'top-down' or 'bottom-up' (ETSU 1995: 6). Top-down approaches generally use aggregated data, for example, of national air pollution emissions or health impacts, to which costs are ascribed, which are then apportioned to the energy sector. The result is an estimate of average costs (as opposed to marginal costs of, say, new generation facilities). Advantages of this approach are that the data requirements are relatively modest and so results can be produced in a wider range of situations. Its main disadvantages include the lack of attention to site-specific environmental impacts and conditions, and the lack of marginal analysis which is required when making new investment decisions.

The bottom-up methodologies generally entail analyses of environmental costs which are more specific to given technologies, sites, demographic and environmental conditions. Data is required from the main stages in the 'impacts pathway': emissions of pollutants, their dispersion and deposition, the sensitivity of receptors to pollution, dose-response relationships, and, finally, an economic valuation of impacts. This category of approaches therefore attempts to construct some kind of 'damage function'. It allows for marginal analysis of new projects, and has the advantage of being more specific to particular power plants and locations. The most serious disadvantage of the damage function approach is that it is very data-intensive, which imposes severe constraints where data gaps are significant.

In the sections which follow, thirteen significant externality studies which have been documented in the literature are summarised briefly. These studies have been undertaken mainly in industrialised countries. The reason for presenting them is less to make comparisons between them or with South Africa than to identify methodological approaches which can inform a South Africa-specific analysis.

## Externality studies in industrialised countries

### The Hohmeyer study in Germany, 1988

Hohmeyer (1988) was responsible for one of the first major attempts at valuing environmental costs in the energy sector, using West German data. This study used a 'top-down' approach: it utilised other studies' estimates of the country's total damage costs attributable to air pollution, then apportioned this to various sources of emissions, including the fossil fuel-based power sector and the nuclear power sector. The study was performed under contract for the Commission for European Communities and was undertaken in the context of governments taking corrective action against market barriers to renewable energy technologies. It concluded that accounting for external effects would improve the competitive position of renewable sources of energy. The valuation estimates produced by the Hohmeyer study are summarised at the end of this section, but it is worth noting that they were highly significant: of the same order of magnitude as private electricity production costs. As a result, the Hohmeyer study received considerable amounts of attention, particularly in Germany (Friedrich & Voss 1993: 114).

In subsequent work, Hohmeyer has extended the scope of the externalities for which valuations have been calculated, and has produced valuations for the emissions of greenhouse gases (Hohmeyer & Gartner 1992). The latter estimates were very significant in relation to other external costs.

### The Pace University study in the United States, 1991

Ottinger et al. (1991) were contracted by the United States Department of Energy and the New York State regulatory authority to review the international literature on the methodologies used to assign monetary costs to environmental externalities, and to present the results of those studies (1991: 13). The intention of the study was to assist utilities, regulatory bodies, legislators, policy analysts and public interest groups in estimating the environmental costs of electricity supply, in the context of integrated resource planning decisions. The Pace study utilised a bottom-up, damage function approach, drawing on numerous studies which had addressed specific aspects of the damage pathway; it undertook no primary data collection of its own.

The environmental costs produced by Ottinger et al. were derived from a spreadsheet-based model which included data on pollution emissions, dispersion, dose-response relationships, and monetary valuation of impacts. Default values for all of these variables were selected on the basis of the existing body of literature. The result of their efforts was an extremely comprehensive report, over 750 pages in length, with estimates of environmental costs for the major impacts for each of seven resource options: coal, oil, natural gas, nuclear, renewable technologies (hydro, solar, wind and biomass facilities), waste-to-energy facilities and demand-side management options. The most important of these results are summarised at the end of this section.

### The Tellus Institute study in Wisconsin, United States, 1991

Bernow et al. (1991) performed a study of the environmental costs of a group of pollutants associated with electricity utilities in Wisconsin state. The context was one of resource planning for utility investment, and estimates of environmental costs were produced for air pollution emissions from several coal-based generation technologies. This study differed from those described above, in that its methodology was not based on the damage function approach, but on the 'regulators' revealed preference' approach. The motivation for this was that information requirements for the damage cost approach were excessive, and instead, the cost of meeting targets for environmental quality as prescribed by regulatory agencies was taken to reflect society's willingness to pay to avoid the risk of those damages (21). The marginal control costs were thus used as a surrogate for marginal damage costs.

Whilst the 'regulators revealed preference' approach avoided the information gathering problems faced by damage function studies, it has been criticised for making the assumption that regulators know what marginal damage costs are and that they make the optimal regulatory decision (ETSU 1995: 7). This logic is argued to be self-referencing, and would automatically equate marginal abatement costs with marginal abatement benefits, since the latter are equal to avoided environmental costs, which in turn are valued at the cost of achieving the regulator's target level of pollution.

### The Pearce et al. study in the United Kingdom, 1992

Pearce and colleagues were contracted by the UK Department of Trade and Industry to survey the social costs of energy production and use (Pearce et al. 1992). This study drew on Ottinger et al. (1991) and other literature, which was used as the basis for making its own estimates of external costs. The approach used was similar to that of Ottinger et al., although it adopted a fuel cycle approach, which meant therefore that it addressed a more complete picture (ETSU 1995: 7). As with the previous studies, Pearce and colleagues did not collect any primary site-specific data and therefore the externality valuations produced are prone to uncertainty and inaccuracy when considering specific sites. More recently, Pearce revised the earlier estimates (1995).

## The Lockwood study in the United Kingdom, 1992

The Parliamentary Office of Science and Technology in the UK commissioned a study undertaken by Lockwood (1992), which was a review, synthesis and extension of the literature on external costs, giving specific attention to the UK. The main sources of literature reviewed were the studies of Hohmeyer and Ottinger et al.. Their methodologies were assessed as being 'broadly correct' and their results in line with those in the literature at the time, although they were criticised on two grounds: their estimates of dose-response relationships (for example, in the case of the impacts of acidic deposition) were not easily generalisable since these are highly site-specific in practice, and secondly, the wide range of estimates attributable to nuclear power was due to extreme uncertainty over the probability of catastrophic accidents. The report did not offer any revised estimates of social costs.

An important element in this study was the consideration given to 'fiscal externalities', in addition to the usual environmental externalities. Fiscal externalities include (primarily) taxes and subsidies which often affect different fuel cycles to varying degrees. The report concluded that coal-based electricity in the UK is taxed by up to 0.95p/kWh (about 5 c/kWh), while nuclear-generated electricity is effectively subsidised by about 0.15 to 0.45 p/kWh (or 0.8 to 2.5 c/kWh) (Lockwood 1992: i). The report also concluded that there was some economic justification, on the basis of external cost estimates, for the incremental installation of flue-gas desulphurisation equipment on coal-fired plant.

## The Friedrich & Voss study in Germany, 1993

The attention which the Hohmeyer study focused on the issue of externalities precipitated many other studies elsewhere, but also prompted others in Germany to analyse the issue. In one such case, Friedrich and Voss scrutinised the methods and data used in the Hohmeyer study, found them to be 'unsuitable' and the corresponding estimates of external costs 'too high' (1993: 114). As a result, they did their own analysis of Germany's external costs in various fuel cycles, with a view also to establishing whether the relative ranking of resource options would change. Their conclusions were that, while the internalisation of externalities could avoid or reduce misallocations of scare economic resources, it would *not* necessarily lead to changes in the competitive positions of coal, nuclear, wind, solar and so on (122).

## *The US-EC external costs of fuel cycles project, 1991-1993*

Following the earlier studies described above, a major project was initiated jointly in 1991 between the US Department of Energy and the European Commission, with the aim of developing an accounting methodology to systematically evaluate external costs of various fuel cycles. The study used a damage function approach and provided an accounting framework within which external costs could be operationalised. A number of research groups from both sides of the Atlantic Ocean contributed to this project, which developed a conceptual and accounting framework for assessing the external costs of various fuel cycles. The first phase of the project was completed in June 1993, and thereafter work continued to be done in the US and Europe, although more independently, since this involved the application of the methodologies in particular contexts. These projects are described separately below.

## *The ExternE study for the European Commission, 1993 and ongoing*

The European Commission supported subsequent phases of the joint US-EC study described above, in the so-called 'ExternE project', covering the period from July 1993 to 1998 (ETSU 1995: 11). The main components of ExternE included the following:

- The methodology which had been developed in the first phase for the coal and nuclear cycles was extended to several other cycles: oil, gas, lignite, hydro, biomass and wind.

- The methodologies were implemented in a number of European states, including the UK, Germany, France, Netherlands, Greece, Portugal, Italy, Spain and Norway (ETSU 1995: 12).

- Software tools for application of the methodology were being developed with a view to allowing application of the approach in local circumstances, including facilities to perform sensitivity analyses. As of mid-1995, these tools were still under development.

Through the process of implementation of the methodology and the development of software tools, the approach has been reviewed and improved.

The principal focus in ExternE has been on the development of a methodology, rather than the calculation of values of external costs. The aim of the methodology is to allow for the calculation of marginal external costs and benefits for a specific power plant, at a specific site and using specified technologies. It adopts a cradle-to-grave view of environmental impacts and thus approximates a life-cycle analysis in cases where upstream impacts (such as coal-mining) are included.

### The US Department of Energy study, 1993-1995

The US portion of the joint US-EC study was led by the Oak Ridge National Laboratory (ORNL) and Resources for the Future (RFF) and was similar in many respects to the ExternE project. A similar but separate series of publications were produced, covering the various fuel cycles and methodological questions (ORNL/RFF 1994a-b, 1995a-e). The methods were also implemented for US conditions; the results of these studies are summarised later in this section. As with the ExternE project, the results of applying the methodology have been criticised by Ottinger (1995) on the grounds that the valuations of external effects were too conservative and failed to adequately account for all external costs. He argued that the values produced would render externalities irrelevant to decision-making, with potentially serious environmental and health consequences.

### The RCG-Tellus study in New York state, 1995

This study, called the New York State Environmental Externalities Cost Study, also utilised the damage cost approach and entailed the development of a user-friendly computer model (called EXMOD) which could be used to calculate external costs for specific electricity resource options (Rowe et al. 1995). The study was supported by a consortium of regulatory and research organisations in New York state, in response to an order by the New York Public Service Commission to develop a methodology to estimate external environmental damages for new and relicensed supply and demand-side management options in the state (Lee 1995: 4). The study therefore had two main components, the first being the development of a methodological tool, and the second being its application to the circumstances prevailing in New York. The results of the valuation exercise were also criticised by Ottinger (1995) on the grounds that the study undervalued or neglected several important categories of external costs. Notably for present purposes, the criticisms were not directed at the EXMOD model, which was singled out as being 'excellent'. The EXMOD methodology is described in more detail later in the report.

### The Schleisner et al. study in Denmark, 1995

A collaborative project was carried out by various institutions in Denmark in order to assess the damage costs of energy production in the country, based on coal-fired, wind, biomass and natural gas power generation facilities. The study used a damage cost approach and relied partly on data collected in the ExternE project described earlier. It included in its scope estimates of damage costs resulting from climate change. External cost estimates for the coal and wind options were reported by Schleisner et al. (1995) and are summarised shortly.

## Developing country studies of external costs

All of the studies described thus far have been undertaken in highly industrialised countries which have their own set of dynamics around environmental and development objectives. Much less work has been undertaken on externalities in developing countries, reflecting partly the relatively lower priority accorded to environmental goals, and partly the smaller role of the electricity generation sector in their economies. This section reviews two investigations of environmental costs which have been undertaken in developing countries.

### The Carnevali and Suarez study in Argentina, 1993

Carnevali and Suarez undertook an economic assessment of the effect of the Argentinean government's energy policies in terms of their environmental impacts (1993: 68). These policies in the 1970s and 1980s encouraged a two-pronged substitution: firstly, hydroelectricity and nuclear energy for conventional thermal energy (mainly coal and oil), and secondly, natural gas for coal and oil. This study, whilst not attempting to place a value on external costs in cents per kWh, did quantify the avoided air pollution emissions as well as the avoided environmental control costs which flowed from the government's substitution policies. It was estimated that the switch to cleaner fuel options, although not motivated by environmental concerns, avoided capital expenditure of about $1 580 million by 1985. This highlighted the need to include environmental considerations in energy investment decisions which are often concerned only with microeconomic criteria.

### The Dutkiewicz and de Villiers study in South Africa, 1993

The only investigation to-date of external costs in South Africa was undertaken by Dutkiewicz and de Villiers (1993) under contract to the National Energy Council (NEC) (which was subsequently disbanded and absorbed into the Department of Mineral and Energy Affairs). The objective of the report was to quantify those external costs for which data was available, for four generation options – coal, nuclear, wind and solar – with a view to assessing whether internalisation of these costs would lead to a re-ranking of the competitiveness of those options (Dutkiewicz & de Villiers 1993: ii). The objective of the study was therefore similar to that of Hohmeyer (1988). The methodology used was a damage cost approach, relying mainly on a review of the international literature on external costs (notably Hohmeyer and Ottinger et al.), supplemented by local data where this was available. The reference year was 1989.

The study noted that there were numerous data gaps, which did not permit the quantification of external costs, although it was suggested that most of these were probably not significant (Dutkiewicz & de Villiers 1993: 14, 40). The cost estimates produced by the study were at the low end of the range of international studies; these are summarised in the following section. The cost estimates, while showing large relative differences between the different fuel cycles, were too small in absolute terms to make any difference to the competitiveness of renewables compared to coal or nuclear (41). A fuller investigation was considered necessary.

# A summary of environmental costs in the international literature

Distinguishing features of the environmental costs produced by the externality studies undertaken to date are the numerical discrepancies and lack of consistency when their results are compared. This uncertainty is sometimes used by sceptics to discount altogether the validity of such attempts. This, however, is an unconstructive and uncritical response, since many of the differences can be accounted for by the varying technical and environmental conditions pertaining to the studies, as well as to methodological differences. It is instructive to summarise the results of valuation studies, both as a point of reference for South African purposes, and in order to highlight the key factors which have accounted for their different results.

The estimates of external environmental costs produced by the major studies reviewed above are summarised in Table 3.1. Of those described above, Tellus (1991) is not included in the table, as its scope was limited to coal-fired combustion, and it used the 'regulators revealed preference' methodology. Its estimates of external costs ranged from 6.4 c/kWh (converted from 1990 dollars) for combined cycle gas turbines, to 16.91 c/kWh for atmospheric fluidized bed combustion technologies (1991: 86). The joint US-EC project is also not included since it focused on the development of methodologies, and valuation was subsequently done in the ORNL/RFF and ExternE projects.

| Study | Fuel cycles[1] | | | | | | |
|---|---|---|---|---|---|---|---|
| | Coal | Nuclear | Gas | Oil | Hydro | Solar | Wind |
| Hohmeyer (1988) | 14.49 to 33.05 | 6.45 to 77.96 | 14.49 to 33.05 | 14.49 to 33.05 | no est. | +2 5.51 to +64.05[2] | +21.01 to +46.12[2] |
| Ottinger et al. (1991) | 24.67 | 12.33 | 5.12 | 11.49 to 28.51 | no est. | 0 to 1.70 | 0 to 0.42 |
| Pearce (1992) | 7.25 to 30.71[3] | 0.31 to 1.84[4] | 2.33 | 34.11 | 0.25 | 0.43 | 0.25 |
| Friedrich & Voss (1993)[5] | 0.87 to 4.65 | 0.06 to 1.35 | no est. | no est. | no est. | 0.16 to 2.69 | 0.08 to 0.83 |
| Dutkiewicz & de Villiers (1993)[6] | 0.93 | 0.26 to 0.80 | no est. | no est. | no est. | 0.01 to 0.05 | 0.01 to 0.04 |
| ORNL/RFF (1994a,b;1995a-e) | 0.21 0.47[7] | 0.08 0.12 | 0.00 0.08 | 0.06 0.08 | 0 0.06[8] | no est. | no est. |
| ExternE (ETSU 1995) | 3.24 7.94[9] | 0.05 1.31[10] | 0.38 | 6.26 | 1.20[11] | no est. | 0.57 to 1.20[12] |
| RCG/Tellus (Rowe et al. 1995) | 1.0113 | 0.0414 | 0.08 | 0.54 | no est. | no est. | 0.0 |
| Schleisner et al. (1995) | 0.73 to 9.52[15] | no est. | no est. | no est. | no est. | no est. | 0.07 to 0.73 |

**Notes**

1. All amounts in 1994 SA cents/kWh, converted from 1994 US cents at a rate of R3.66/$1, and from 1993 German Marks at R1.98/DM1; where relevant, amounts in Rands have been adjusted using a 10% annual inflation factor.
2. + denotes an external benefit.
3. Estimates for a 'new' and 'old' plant respectively.
4. High estimate reflects risk averse valuation of health impacts of nuclear disaster.
5. Estimates are for 4000 full load hours p.a., and include external costs of back-up system.
6. Estimates originally in 1989 Rands, annual adjustment used of 10%.
7. Estimates for plants in the rural south-west and south-east US respectively.
8. Estimates for retrofit on existing dams in Kentucky, and diversion project in Washington state, respectively.
9. All but 0.02 c/kWh was due to the aesthetic value of a waterfall, which was estimated in a contingent valuation study.
10. Estimates using a 3% and 0% discount rate respectively.
11. The first estimate was for a site at West Burton, UK; the second was for Laufen, Germany.
12. Estimates for various sites in the UK.
13. Estimates are for a rural site in New York state.
14. For a boiling water reactor, rather than pressurised water reactor.
15. Estimates are for a 'conventional coal-fired plant' defined as a 350 MW plant with desulphurisation and de-NOx equipment.

**Table 3-1** Fuel cycle external costs (in c/kWh) estimated by various studies *(adapted from Lee 1995: 5; Friedrich & Voss 1993: 121; Dutkiewicz & de Villiers 1993: 41; Schleisner et al. 1995)*

For purposes of this report, the most important fuel cycles are coal and, secondarily, nuclear; nonetheless, it is interesting to compare the external costs of these cycles with others, which becomes especially relevant when making decisions about new investments with various resource options. As would be expected, renewable options fare much better than fossil fuel and nuclear fuel cycles, with large relative differences in external costs. Of all fuel cycles, coal had the consistently highest external cost, with the exception of nuclear in Hohmeyer's study and oil in Pearce's study.

It is evident from the table that there are wide variances in the numbers produced by the studies. These differences are due at least as much to different methodologies, as they are to different physical, technical and environmental conditions prevailing in the respective case studies.

Upon closer inspection of externalities in the coal cycle, it is apparent that the studies can be grouped into two categories, based on the order of magnitude of their results. The first comprises the three earlier studies – Hohmeyer, Ottinger and Pearce – which produced external cost estimates in the range of 7.3 c/kWh to 33.1 c/kWh. The second group of studies, which were all conducted post-1992, produced lower estimates, in the range of 0.21 c/kWh to 9.52 c/kWh. In analysing the differences in these studies, the following main factors may be identified (partly drawn from Lee 1995: 2-3):

- *Methodology:* While all the studies summarised in the table used the damage cost approach, they used different methods to obtain data on components in the impact pathway. The earlier studies generally used other studies' estimates of pollution emissions and impacts, and multiplied these by economic values to calculate damage costs. The second group of studies, on the other hand, either used more complex and specific methods to collect data on pollution emissions, dispersion and impacts, such as atmospheric models and dose-response functions, or they used lower valuations. In practice, the effect has been that the earlier studies used higher estimates of emissions, concentrations and impacts.

- *Emission factors:* The earlier studies' emissions factors (measured in tons of pollutant per GWh of electricity generated) were considerably higher than in recent studies, sometimes by a factor of ten. This is partly due to technical differences in the plants which were addressed, in that more recent studies have selected newer plants which have better environmental performance in general, and, in some specific cases, with desulphurisation and other control equipment.

- *Sulphate and nitrate aerosols:* The older studies contain different assumptions about emissions of $SO_2$ (from which damaging sulphate aerosols are formed) and about their dispersion in the atmosphere, which lead to higher external cost valuations. $SO_2$-related externalities accounted for 60% of total externalities in Ottinger et al.'s work, and 75% in Hohmeyer's study, both of which are considerably higher than the more recent studies.

- *Climate change damages:* In earlier studies, fairly high values were attributed to damages caused by climate change (impacts include, for example, sea level rise, increased drought and climatic extremes), whereas in more recent studies, analysts have argued that there is too much scientific uncertainty about the impacts of climate change (without questioning its likelihood of occurring) to make meaningful estimates of damage costs. Recent studies have, in turn, been criticised for understating the likely scale of those impacts by avoiding their valuation (Ottinger 1995: 4).

If any conclusions are to be drawn from these international studies, then the first would be that external costs can be significant in absolute terms, as well as in relative terms when comparing alternative fuel cycles. International experience therefore points to the need to investigate externalities in South Africa's power sector. A second observation would be that it is important not to take external costs simply at face value, but that they need to be evaluated in the specific contexts in which they were calculated. Thus it is important that the values summarised above are not simply applied uncritically to the South African situation, but that local circumstances be taken into account as far as possible. Finally, it is important that assumptions and methodologies are made explicit in order that results of the valuation exercise can be appraised in the appropriate context. Equally, it is important that all limitations in the valuation exercise be made apparent.

# 4

# Externalities in South Africa's electricity industry

It could be expected that South Africa's electricity industry would have fairly significant environmental impacts, if only by virtue of its absolute size. These impacts, however, need to be evaluated in their economic, political and social contexts in order to make appropriate policy decisions about their management. This chapter reviews the main categories of environmental impact arising from the coal and nuclear generation sectors, while the following chapter assesses the economic implications of the most important of these externalities.

## The impact pathway approach

Given that there is a wide range of environmental impacts arising from the energy sector, it is necessary to adopt a systematic approach to their identification and evaluation. The method used in this study, which has been used in the majority of international externalities studies, is the impact pathway or damage function approach. This approach is illustrated conceptually in Figure 4.1.

The damage function approach entails the identification and quantification of environmental and other damages arising at each stage in the fuel cycle: from the extraction of raw materials (such as coal or uranium), to their transport and processing, to their consumption in power stations, to the impacts of waste products arising in the electricity generation process, and their impacts on human health and amenity, and on the physical and natural environments.

It is evident from Figure 4.1 that the impact pathway approach corresponds with the real-world steps in the fuel cycle; thus an externalities study which succeeds in quantifying the impacts at each stage of the fuel cycle will have a reasonably realistic correlation to the actual impacts arising from that cycle. A successful impact pathway approach will yield results which are more realistic than other externality methodologies,[1] and will therefore be of more use for

---

1     Less direct methods include, for example, the 'regulators' revealed preference' approach, or 'top down' externality approaches, both of which were described in an earlier chapter.

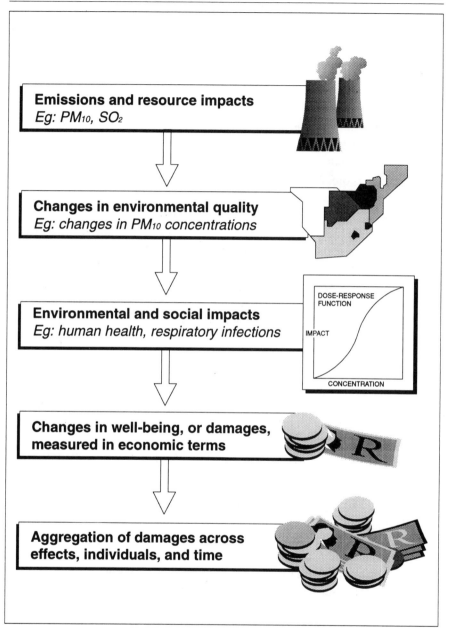

**Figure 4.1** The damage function approach for power station
emissions
(after Rowe et al. 1995: 3)

policy-making. The damage function approach is generally regarded as the preferred approach to assessing environmental externalities (Rowe et al. 1995: 2). It is important to note, however, that the damage function approach is also subject to weaknesses, most of which are related to the fact that it attempts to quantify realistic processes and events. These limitations include the following (Rowe et al.: 2):

- Firstly, the approach is highly data-intensive, since information is required about each step in the impact pathway. As a result, such studies, if they are to be comprehensive and scientifically sound, are costly.

- Secondly, professional judgements are required about the most appropriate data to use, since there are often conflicting views in the externalities literature, and the result can be sensitive to these judgements.

- If there are omissions, inaccuracies or biases in the data, these can be compounded throughout the assessment chain, thereby limiting the usefulness of the end results.

- Finally, the damage function approach is fairly complex and draws upon a number of disciplines, which can render such studies inaccessible to the wider audience which may be interested in their results.

Whilst the data requirements of a comprehensive impact pathway assessment are formidable, there is a relatively large body of relevant information which makes it possible to employ the approach in South Africa. The externalities modelling tool which is used in this study for air pollution impacts, EXMOD (described in more detail in Chapter 5), has the important feature of making its assumptions relatively transparent and, more particularly, it accommodates uncertainty in an explicit fashion.

A further important characteristic of the damage function approach is that it allows for the analysis to proceed as far down the impact chain as the decision-maker chooses. Thus, for instance, if there is uncertainty (or ethical disagreement) over the valuation of human health effects or crop damages from air pollution, then it is possible to use the information about physical impacts as the basis for decision-making; in other words, it is entirely possible to stop short of the economic valuation of externalities if the decision-maker chooses. Moreover, provided these input assumptions are made explicit, it is possible for users to perform sensitivity analyses or enter alternative values for particular variables.

For present purposes, this study focuses on the most important steps in the impact pathway of the coal fuel cycle. Given time and information constraints, it is not possible to evaluate externalities at every step in the chain; moreover, beyond a certain point, there will be diminishing returns from widening the scope of the study to include less serious environmental and other impacts. Furthermore, a degree of judgement is required in making decisions regarding which externalities are potentially significant and which are not. Consequently, a classification system is proposed for this study, which will make explicit the criteria used in determining the scope of the quantification exercise. Environmental impacts are classified according to the following three categories:

- *Class One impacts* are environmental impacts which are potentially serious, *and* for which sufficient information exists to permit an estimate of their economic value.

- *Class Two impacts* are potentially serious, but for which there is insufficient data to permit an economic assessment of external costs within an acceptable range of certainty.

- *Class Three impacts* are impacts which, on balance of evidence and probability, are not likely to be highly material in relation to other impacts, and therefore no attempt is made to quantify them in economic terms; alternatively, the environmental costs of these impacts have already been substantially internalised.

The sections which follow, therefore, describe those environmental impacts in the coal and nuclear fuel cycles which are viewed as potentially significant, with a view to assessing the state of knowledge about each, whether they are already internalised or remain external, and whether there is sufficient information to permit their economic values to be estimated. The final section of this chapter will summarise the classification of impacts adopted in this study.

# Externalities in South Africa's coal fuel cycle

Environmental impacts arise at most stages in the coal fuel cycle. These impacts are subject to varying levels of management and attempts to ameliorate them; in other words, some of these impacts are already fully or partially internalised into the pricing structure of coal and electricity. This section is concerned primarily with identifying those impacts which remain 'external' to the market, and which are potentially significant. In considering the coal fuel cycle, the following impacts may be identified:

- occupational health effects in coal mining;
- air and water pollution from coal mining;
- water consumption in power generation;
- air pollution from power generation: health impacts;
- air pollution from power generation: impacts of acidic deposition;
- air pollution from power generation: visibility impacts;
- water quality impacts from power generation;
- greenhouse gas emissions from power generation.

Numerous other impacts arise in the generation of electricity from coal, in addition to those described above: for example, the health impacts of electromagnetic fields (EMFs) around high-voltage transmission lines, the loss of productive land above underground mines because of subsidence, and the aesthetic impacts of large power stations and transmission lines in rural areas. Whilst any number of such impacts may have significant environmental or social impacts in their specific or local contexts, they are not considered in any detail in this study, either because they are not significant in aggregate on a national scale, or because their costs have already been substantially internalised.

Each of the impacts listed above will be assessed in more detail in this chapter, and will be quantified in economic terms in the next chapter.

## Occupational health effects in coal mining

Workers in coal mines are exposed to a number of risks. These include rock falls, methane explosions, transport accidents and accidents in the handling of materials, which may result in immediate injury or death. A second category of occupational risks results from prolonged exposure of workers over a number of years to air pollution resulting from mining activities, and illnesses such as emphysema and pneumonia occur.

A Commission of Enquiry, the 'Leon Commission' reported in mid-1995 on the state of health and safety on South Africa's gold and coal mines. The general tone of the Commission's report was sharply critical of the health and safety management in the country's gold and coal mines, and highlighted the high morbidity and mortality rates compared to other major mining countries. This was more especially the case in the gold mines, which generally operate at much deeper levels than coal mines.[2] The Leon Commission reported on the number of injuries and fatalities in the mining industry for the period 1984 to 1993; the data for coal mines is summarised in Table 4.1.

This data represents averages of open-cast and underground coal mines; the rates for these types of mines, however, differ, as do accident rates from one mine to another. No data was available for the present study regarding the actual number of incidents on the mines serving Eskom's power stations. Nonetheless, this can be calculated from available data sources. The Leon Commission reported that there were 47 injuries and nine fatalities on open-cast mines during 1993 (1995: 22). Total coal production at open-cast mines was in the region of 35% of the total (Raimondo et al. 1995: 12), equivalent to 64 Mt, which means that the fatality rate on occupational mines was 0.14 per Mt, and the injury rate 0.73 per Mt.

---

2   Ironically, the release of the Leon Commission report coincided with a serious accident at the Vaal Reefs Gold Mine, in which 104 miners were killed when their lift-cage dropped hundreds of metres down a mine shaft.

| Year | Coal mined (Mt) | Fatalities | | | Injuries | | |
|---|---|---|---|---|---|---|---|
| | | Number | Per 1000 workers | Per Mt mined | Number | Per 1000 workers | Per Mt mined |
| 1984 | 162.9 | 73 | 0.63 | 0.45 | 840 | 7.20 | 4.94 |
| 1985 | 173.5 | 93 | 0.78 | 0.54 | 806 | 6.80 | 4.65 |
| 1986 | 176.7 | 66 | 0.55 | 0.37 | 709 | 5.90 | 4.01 |
| 1987 | 176.6 | 121 | 1.05 | 0.69 | 550 | 4.86 | 3.11 |
| 1988 | 181.4 | 53 | 0.50 | 0.29 | 435 | 4.07 | 2.40 |
| 1989 | 176.3 | 54 | 0.52 | 0.31 | 361 | 3.50 | 2.05 |
| 1990 | 174.8 | 50 | 0.52 | 0.29 | 404 | 4.21 | 2.31 |
| 1991 | 178.2 | 42 | 0.56 | 0.24 | 361 | 4.80 | 2.06 |
| 1992 | 174.4 | 46 | 0.66 | 0.26 | 339 | 5.17 | 1.94 |
| 1993 | 182.2 | 90 | 1.71 | 0.49 | 279 | 5.32 | 1.53 |
| Average | 175.7 | 69 | 0.75 | 0.39 | 508 | 5.18 | 2.90 |

**Table 4.1**   Accident data for South African coal mines, 1984 to 1993
(Leon Commission 1995:19; Minerals Bureau 1994: 32)

Accident rates for underground mines can therefore be estimated by removing the incidents attributed to open-cast mines from the data in Table 4.1. There is no clear trend in the fatality data shown in the Table, and so the average for the ten-year period will be used: 69 fatalities per year. If nine fatalities occurred on open-cast mines, then there were 60 deaths on underground mines; this is equivalent to a fatality rate of 0.51 per Mt. For injury data, there is a clear downward trend in the rate of injuries over the ten-year period 1984-1993, and so the ten-year average could overstate current accident rates. Consequently, the average for the last five years will be used, which amounts to an average of 349 injuries per annum, or 2.95 injuries per Mt mined in underground operations.

Of the nine coal power stations, four are open-cast, three are underground, and two have a mixture of both, in roughly equal proportions (Du Plooy 1995). From this, and on the basis of electricity generated at each power station, the split between coal sourced at underground mines compared to open-cast mines can be estimated at around 43 : 57 for 1994. Fatality and injury rates can therefore be calculated for coal mines serving Eskom's power stations; these are summarised in Table 4.2.

| | % split | Fatality rate (per mt) | Injury rate (per mt) |
|---|---|---|---|
| Underground | 43% | 0.51 | 2.95 |
| Open-cast | 57% | 0.14 | 0.73 |
| Total/ weighted av. | 100% | 0.30 | 1.68 |

**Table 4.2**  Calculated accident rates for underground and open-cast
mines supplying Eskom

Thus an average of 0.30 fatalities and 1.68 injuries occur for every million tons of coal mined for purposes of power generation. On average, 0.52 kg of coal is used for each kWh of electricity generated (Eskom 1995a: 54), so this translates into 0.156 fatalities and 0.874 injuries per thousand GWh of electricity produced. Applying this rate to 1994 electricity production of 149 443 GWh, then a total of 23 workers would have died in coal mines supplying Eskom in that year, and a further 131 would have been injured.

The nature of injuries sustained by coal miners varies widely, from relatively minor injuries to permanently disabling ones. A breakdown of the kind of injuries on coal mines averaged over 1993 and 1994, obtained from the Government Mining Engineer's office, shows that the main kinds of injuries were of the following kinds: arm, hand and finger injuries: 37%; legs and feet: 36%; trunk: 13%; head and neck: 9%; with the remainder being unspecified or multiple injuries (GME 1995). The definition of 'reportable injuries' includes those incurred in accidents of a serious nature where the worker cannot work for 48 hours or more, as well as those occurring in the 'normal course of duties' where the person is away from work for 14 days or more. The range of periods for which an injured person cannot work obviously varies widely, depending on the kind of injury. According to the GME, most reportable injuries lead to considerably more than 14 days of lost work, although no data was available on the exact number of lost days. According to Rand Mutual Association (which pays compensation to injured workers), injuries vary from six to eight weeks for broken legs or arms, to eight to 24 months for more serious spinal injuries. Since over 70% of injuries during 1994 were to limbs, a central estimate of eight weeks for injuries will be used for this study. Low and high estimates are taken as four and twelve weeks respectively; these will be accounted for in the valuation exercise in Chapter Five.

In addition, cash compensation is paid to workers according to a standard scale of benefits, in terms of the Compensation for Occupational Injuries and Diseases Act, in respect of all reportable injuries and deaths. These will also be included in the valuation exercise in Chapter Five.

With respect to chronic and acute respiratory illnesses resulting from prolonged exposure to air pollution, evidence heard by the Leon Commission suggests that these effects are significant (1995: 16-17). The most common effects are tuberculosis, emphysema, hearing impairment, pneumoconiosis and silicosis. However, there have been no published studies of the pollution levels to which workers are exposed, nor of the dose-response relationships applicable to coal miners. Quantification of these impacts, in either physical or economic terms, is therefore not possible in the present study, and hence these occupational health impacts are accorded a Class Two classification.

In addition to the obvious questions raised by the above statistics about the safety management policies of the mining industry – which are beyond the scope of this study – the relevant question for present purposes relates to whether the health and safety risks which are faced by coal miners are reflected in their wages (and therefore the prices of coal and, ultimately, electricity). In other words, are coal miners compensated for the occupational health risks they face in their employment, which, as the above data shows, are not trivial?

Externality studies in some countries have focused on wage premiums as a means of deriving valuations of worker's 'willingness to accept compensation' for negative environmental or occupational conditions – the so-called 'hedonic wage pricing' approach (Freeman 1993: 421). The logic behind this is that workers would not accept work under dangerous or hazardous conditions unless they were adequately compensated for those risks, and that this premium therefore can be used as an indication of their 'valuation' of the environmental risks. All other things equal, in a free market situation (that is, with conditions of free bargaining, full information, etc), the environmental risks would be fully internalised into worker's higher wages. However, the South African labour market does not even remotely approximate an idealised 'efficient market', as evidenced most significantly by a formal employment rate of only around 50%. In this context, it is evident that workers are not in a strong position to bargain for full compensation for occupational risks.

The more difficult task of applying economic values to these impacts is addressed in detail in Chapter 5. For the present, however, the occurrence of deaths and injuries will be classified as a Class One impact, since sufficient information exists regarding the rates of injury and death to quantify them. In the case of chronic and acute illnesses resulting from exposure to air pollution on the mines, however, insufficient information exists to quantify the economic value of this externality, and so this is classified as a Class Two impact.

### Air and water pollution from coal mining

Coal mining is undertaken in South Africa through four methods: board and pillar, open-cast mining, long-wall mining and pillar extraction (Raimondo et al. 1995: 12). Of these, the first two dominate, accounting for 50% and 35% respectively of total coal extracted in 1987. The air and water impacts of coal mining vary widely, depending in the first instance upon the kind of mine concerned.

In general, Eskom secures its coal from mines located adjacent to the power stations. These mines are owned by private sector mining houses, which have generally entered into long-term contracts with Eskom to supply its needs over the lifetime of the power station (30 to 40 years on average). These long-term contracts have advantages for mining houses in that they are assured of consumer demand for their output, and for Eskom in that it can secure favourable prices for coal, which is the main variable cost in the generation of electricity. In 1994 Eskom paid an average of just under R30 per ton of coal burnt (1995a: 54). By comparison, the average price of exported coal (which is generally of a higher quality than Eskom's coal) was R85 per ton in 1993, local coal prices for wholesale industrial consumers averaged R39 per ton, and at the end of the distribution chain for low-income households, retail prices were in the region of R200 per ton (Minerals Bureau 1994: 33; Palmer Development Group 1995: 21). These price variances are attributable largely to the costs of transportation and distribution. This serves to emphasise, then, the cost advantages Eskom enjoys by securing its coal supplies from mines close enough to its power stations to be able to transport coal from the mine's stockpile to the furnaces, by conveyor belt. In many other countries, coal is delivered to power stations by rail, which, given the bulky nature of the commodity, adds considerably to the cost of electricity.

To the extent that Eskom purchases its coal from private sector mining companies, it cannot be said that its coal is subsidised. However, there may be implicit costs in the coal mining cycle which are not accounted for in the operations of mining companies. The main external costs – over and above the costs of ill-health and mortality in the work force, described above – arise from air pollution and water pollution in the mining process and related activities. In particular, three categories of impact arise:

- Open-cast mining is responsible for increased levels of dust and airborne particulate matter caused by blasting, vehicular traffic and movement of coal and waste products.

- Large dumps of discard coal are prone to spontaneous combustion when not compacted sufficiently and, where this occurs, significant amounts of air pollution can be emitted for long periods of time.

- Water supplies in the proximity of coal dumps and open mine pits can be degraded by chemical run-off, thereby affecting ground water supplies as well.

The relevant question for present purposes is whether there are significant and measurable economic costs associated with any of these impacts and, if there are, whether they are internalised or not.

With respect to the air quality impacts described in the first two points above, it appears that coal mines and their dumps have historically made a significant contribution to ambient pollution levels in the coal-mining areas (Annegarn 1995: 15). However, there is no data regarding emissions from specific mines or dumps, which makes it difficult to apportion emissions between the various coal-consuming sectors.

At the same time, the number of burning mine dumps has been reduced considerably in the past few years due to better management practices on the part of the relevant mining companies (Annegarn 1995: 15). This suggests that the environmental costs of mine management are increasingly being internalised. One of the mechanisms through which this takes place is the 'Environmental Management Plan' which all mines are required to prepare and submit to the Department of Mineral and Energy Affairs before they receive a licence to commence mining activities (Raimondo et al.: 29). Prospective mining companies are also required to lodge a bond (a monetary deposit) up-front, to insure against the future costs of rehabilitation and decommissioning.

With respect to the water quality impacts of leaching and ground-water pollution, there is minimal data on which to base an assessment of any economic costs which may arise. Although it is not feasible to estimate external costs in the present study, it is important to note that the issues of water quality and water scarcity are receiving increasing policy attention at all levels of government.

For purposes of this study, these impacts fall both into Class Two, to the extent that the air and water quality impacts of coal mining may be serious, but that there is a large degree of uncertainty over their extent; and into Class Three, to the extent that they have already been internalised through environmental management procedures.

## Water consumption in power generation

Coal-powered electricity is a fairly significant consumer of water in South Africa. Water is an integral part of the thermal power generation process, being used not only (as steam) to drive the turbines which generate electricity, but also to cool down the steam in large cooling towers. Most of Eskom's power stations utilise conventional wet-cooling processes, although two, Kendal and Matimba, use dry-cooling processes which were pioneered by Eskom.[3] Average water consumption in each of the coal power stations is shown in Table 4.3.

---

3    In these power stations, the cooling towers utilise massive fans to blow air onto hot water pipes to cool them down.

| | Water consumed | | Average price (R/m³) |
| --- | --- | --- | --- |
| | Total (million m³) | Per unit (l/kWh | |
| Arnot | 8.875 | 1.76 | 0.55 |
| Duvha | 41.009 | 1.71 | 0.59 |
| Hendrina | 27.188 | 1.69 | 0.40 |
| Kendal | 3.667 | J.16 | 1.78 |
| Kriel | 32.910 | 1.97 | 0.79 |
| Lethabo | 31.624 | 1.87 | 0.12 |
| Matimba | 4.249 | 0.18 | 0.50 |
| Matla | 34.696 | 2.10 | 1.23 |
| Tutuka | 35.239 | 1.96 | 0.66 |
| Total/average | 219.457 | 1.43 | 0.66 |

**Table 4.3**   Water consumption in Eskom's coal-powered stations, 1994 *(Fraser 1995)*

Water costs represent a small fraction of Eskom's total operating costs: in the region of 1.8% of direct operating costs (excluding depreciation and finance charges) (calculated from Eskom 1995a: 41). This, however, understates the importance of water as an input into the electricity generation process – it is an essential raw material, underlined by the fact that Eskom was directly involved in the construction or financing of several dams, long before other consumers demanded water in those areas.

As in the case of coal, Eskom has benefited from water prices which have been low and stable over time. There is a wide range of pricing contracts in place with respect to Eskom's water purchases, each dependent upon the specific source of supply. In general, Eskom purchases its water from the Department of Water Affairs and Forestry (DWAF), and pays on the basis of the historic costs of supplying that water, as distinct from the marginal cost of supplying water. Importantly, the cost of supplying water is dependent primarily on the capital costs of constructing the necessary infrastructure. This means that if historic costing is used as a basis for water pricing, and the capital infrastructure was constructed some time ago, then the price of water will be much lower than the cost of supplying an additional unit of water today (the 'marginal cost'). This, together with the varying sources of supply for Eskom's power stations, accounts for both the range of water prices and the relatively low prices in some cases. Lethabo power station, for instance, draws its water from the Vaal River which was dammed in the early 1900s; hence its water price is considerably lower than the marginal cost of new water supplies.

Since this appears to be an important environmental impact, and there is relatively good data regarding the current consumption and pricing regime, this issue is classified as a Class One environmental impact. Alternative water pricing scenarios and their impact on electricity tariffs are considered in Chapter Five.

## Air pollution from power generation: health impacts

The evaluation of the health impacts from power station emissions is one of the more complex, but important externalities to be considered. Quantification of health impacts requires information for four major steps in the impact pathway:

- the quantities of pollution emitted by power stations;
- the dispersion and ultimate deposition of those pollutants;
- human health responsiveness to various exposures (doses) of pollution;
- the valuation of increased morbidity and mortality.

Each of these steps is addressed below, except for the last, which is dealt with in the next chapter.

### Quantity of pollution emitted by power stations
The coals used in South Africa's power stations are generally of relatively poor quality, since the highest grades are exported. The average ash, sulphur and energy content of coals used by Eskom varies widely, as shown in Table 4.4.

| | Ash content (%) | Sulphur content (%) | Energy content (MJ/kg) |
|---|---|---|---|
| Arnot | 21 | 1.02 | 22.3 |
| Hendrina | 26 | 1.08 | 2.5 |
| Kendal | 24 | 0.85 | 22.0 |
| Kriel | 31 | 1.11 | 19.2 |
| Lethabo | 26 | 0.88 | 20.8 |
| Matimba | 39 | 0.59 | 15.2 |
| Matla | 32 | 1.26 | 18.5 |
| Duvha | 24 | 1.21 | 20.9 |
| Tutuka | 25 | 1.41 | 21.0 |

**Table 4.4**   Average ash, sulphur and energy content of coal used in Eskom's power stations, 1994
*(Source: Eskom Generation group)*

It is evident that the ash content is uniformly high, ranging from 21% at Arnot power station, to 39% at Lethabo; the latter also has the lowest calorific value (energy content), at 15.2 MJ per kilogram of coal. It is significant to note that, with such a low energy content, 'coal' could not be used in any conventional commercial or domestic process.[4] Thus, electricity is being generated from a product which would otherwise have little or no economic value.

The negative side of this is that, all other things being equal, particulate emissions and ash production are relatively high. As a consequence, Eskom's pollution control policy has been concerned primarily with the control of particulate emissions. All of its coal-power stations currently in operation utilise electro-static precipitators (ESPs) to remove the bulk of particulate emissions from flue gases. These typically operate with an efficiency of around 90-99.7% (Tilley & Keir 1994), although it is important to note that it is the finest particles (that is, with the smallest diameter) which present the greatest potential health hazard, since it is these which are small enough to be respirable.[5]

A second technological option which is often used by electricity utilities internationally, entails the use of bag filters to increase the portion of particulates which are removed from exhaust gases. Where bag filters are used successfully, in combination with ESPs, efficiencies of 99.99% are possible (Hanson 1992). Eskom has installed bag filters on a trial basis in some of its power stations, as denoted in Table 4.5.

Eskom's air pollution control policy has a further dimension, to address the particular atmospheric conditions prevailing in the Mpumalanga Highveld: a strong inversion layer which inhibits the dispersal of ground-level or low-level emissions, especially during winter months (Tyson et al. 1988). As a result, the newer power stations have tall chimney stacks, so that emissions penetrate the inversion layer and are released into the upper atmosphere. The effects of this will be described shortly.

A final point to note in relation to Eskom's air pollution policy, is that it has decided that desulphurisation and denitrification technologies are not warranted. Thus, apart from the tall stack policy, no active measures are taken to reduce the emissions of sulphur dioxide or nitrogen oxides. This is an issue which has received much attention in recent years, although there has been no systematic investigation of the costs and benefits of respective pollution control options. This report will return to this issue later.

Particulate, sulphur dioxide and nitrogen oxide emissions from Eskom's coal power stations in 1994 were as shown in Table 4.5.

---

4    Indeed, this coal cannot even be ignited with a blow-torch!

5    Particulate matter with a diameter of 10 μm (microns) or less is usually regarded as being in the respirable range (hence the label PM10).

| | Bag filters | TSP emissions | | SO₂ emissions | | NOx emissions | |
|---|---|---|---|---|---|---|---|
| | | kt | kg/MWh | kt | kg/MWh | kt | kg/MWh |
| Arnot | 3 (of 6) units | 11.00 | 2.41 | 35.8 | 7.86 | 26.3 | 5.77 |
| Duvha | 3 (of 6) units | 8.17 | 0.37 | 180.3 | 8.21 | 136.7 | 6.22 |
| Hendrina | none | 49.70 | 4.19 | 90.5 | 7.62 | 72.9 | 6.14 |
| Kendal | none | 4.63 | 0.24 | 167.8 | 8.65 | 123.2 | 6.35 |
| Kriel | none | 10.56 | 0.79 | 103.9 | 7.76 | 126.5 | 9.44 |
| Lethabo | none | 5.45 | 0.31 | 123.0 | 6.89 | 143.1 | 8.01 |
| Matimba | none | 22.58 | 1.00 | 193.8 | 8.54 | 92.4 | 4.07 |
| Matla | none | 4.54 | 0.24 | 149.4 | 7.97 | 130.9 | 6.99 |
| Tutuka | none | 5.79 | 0.33 | 122.2 | 6.97 | 108.9 | 6.21 |
| *Total/av.* | | 122.42 | 0.84 | 1166.7 | 7.88 | 960.9 | 6.49 |

**Table 4.5**  Total suspended particulate (TSP), sulphur dioxide and nitrogen oxide emissions by Eskom's power stations in 1994

This data represents emissions for 1994 as calculated by Eskom; it should be noted that there is no independent monitoring or measurement of emissions by an environmental authority acting principally in the interests of public health. Eskom's power stations are governed by Registration Certificates, which are issued by the Chief Air Pollution Control Officer (CAPCO), in terms of which maximum permissible emission rates are specified. Transgressions of these limits, however, such as occurred at Hendrina power station, do not lead to direct penalties or costs; in the case of Hendrina during 1994, the CAPCO granted the utility a 'temporary exemption' after 'taking circumstances into account'.

Before addressing the dispersal of pollution from power stations, it is important to note another source of air pollution which is not accounted for in the emissions data quoted above, namely pollution originating from the ash dumps at power stations. The combustion of coal in power stations, much of it with a relatively high ash content, unavoidably leads to extremely large quantities of ash production. Some 22 million tons of ash was produced by Eskom's power stations in 1994, of which about 3% was re-used for cement or brick-making (Eskom 1995b: 23). This translates into a continuous production rate of 42 tons of ash per minute.

Eskom's policy is to dispose of this ash in ash dams or on ash dumps, on land owned by itself, and to minimise the amount of ash liberated into the atmosphere by covering the dumps with grasses and other vegetation where possible. In the critical period before vegetation can stabilise the dumps, waste water is used to reduce the amount of dust which can be blown into the air. Inevitably, however, particularly in windy conditions, significant amounts of dust can originate from these dumps. There is little quantitative data about the amount of pollution which so arises, and so it cannot be included in the present analysis. However, it is clear that the exclusion of this source of pollution from the air quality modelling exercise will understate the contribution of power stations to ambient pollution levels. Moreover, the fact that these ash dumps are at or close to ground level, means that their impact is relatively greater than the impact of emissions from tall chimney stacks. Consequently this source of pollution is not considered any further in this study, and is classified as a Class Two impact.

*Atmospheric conditions and dispersal of pollution*
The quantity of pollution emitted by power facilities is the first main link in the electricity generation part of the impact pathway. The next step implicit in the damage function approach concerns what happens to those pollutants after they are emitted – that is, how they are dispersed in the atmosphere and where they are deposited. For this to be assessed, information is required regarding two key variables:

- physical emission characteristics, such as the height of chimney stacks, and the speed, volume and temperature of flue gas emissions;
- atmospheric conditions, including wind patterns (derived from long-term data), mixing heights and atmospheric stability.

With respect to the first item, data has been collected for each of Eskom's nine coal power stations which were operating in 1994 (this data is reported in Appendix 1). The most significant factor to note is that all of Eskom's power stations have relatively tall chimney stacks of 200 metres or more, with the exception of Arnot (193 metres) and Hendrina (110 metres). This is consistent with the Eskom policy described earlier – in the absence of technologies to reduce sulphur emissions and given that significant quantities of particulate matter are emitted, the chimneys are designed to penetrate the inversion layer, which would otherwise have trapped those pollutants close to the ground before they could be diluted.

With respect to data on atmospheric conditions, long-term surface wind data averaged over a period of ten to twenty years was drawn from Weather Bureau sources for fifteen stations in South Africa and two in Namibia (Weather Bureau 1975). Average frequency distributions for sixteen wind vectors (N, NNW, NW, WNW, W and so on) in various speed classes were obtained. This data, together with the technical power station data described above, was used in atmospheric models contained within the EXMOD model.

The results of the air pollution dispersal and valuation exercise will be described in the next chapter. It is worth briefly reviewing, here, the state of information about pollution levels on the Mpumalanga Highveld. Once again, most of the data on pollution levels in this region is derived from monitoring undertaken by Eskom's own scientists, as there is no regulatory agency in South Africa equipped to do this.[6] Eskom has operated a monitoring network in the Mpumalanga province since 1979, with various site changes having taken place over that period. Data is available for several key pollutants: sulphur dioxide, nitrogen oxides, particulates and ozone. Data on concentrations for each of these pollutants is summarised briefly below.

Sulphur dioxide levels over the past decade were reported to be generally well within annual guideline levels, with the average over the period 1979-1986 being around 26 $\mu gm^{-3}$ (range 9 to 41 $\mu gm^{-3}$) (Turner et al. 1990: 5, Tyson et al. 1988: 46). The Department of Health annual guideline, by comparison, is 78 $\mu gm^{-3}$. However, there were more frequent exceedances of guidelines over shorter (hourly and daily levels) monitoring periods. Whilst long-term trends showed an increase in average $SO_2$ levels over the period 1979-1983, corresponding with the commissioning of new power stations during that period (Turner 1987), Eskom reported that the trend was reversed after 1986. The most recent results from the utility's monitoring network, for 1993, reported no exceedances of $SO_2$ health guidelines at its six monitoring stations (Rorich & Turner 1994: 6).

Pollution data for nitrogen oxides suggests that this pollutant does not represent a major problem: long-term concentrations in the 1980s were around 15 $\mu gm^{-3}$ compared to the national long-term guideline of 376 $\mu gm^{-3}$ (Lennon & Turner 1992: 3). Results for 1993 showed that pollution levels were below guideline values, although short-term peaks were not insignificant (Rorich & Turner: 6).

Particulate concentrations in the Mpumalanga Highveld over the period 1979 to 1983 were well below guidelines, at around 17 $\mu gm^{-3}$ compared to the annual guideline of 150 $\mu gm^{-3}$ (Turner et al.: 5). According to Eskom, its power stations were responsible for around 20% of ambient particulate concentrations, compared to 46% from smouldering coal dumps and local industries – due to the fact that its emissions were better diluted than low-level emissions. The results for 1993 showed no major changes to this situation (Rorich & Turner: 7).

---

6    Eskom has contracted consultants at various stages to audit its monitoring system, and it has generally been satisfied with the results.

Finally, Eskom's monitoring of pollution levels for ozone found that hourly, daily, monthly and annual guidelines were frequently surpassed during the period 1983 to 1988 (Turner et al.: 20, 23). Annual averages were two to three times the annual guideline of 20 $\mu gm^{-3}$ and the trend was increasing. The significance of this is that high levels of ozone can cause direct damage to crops and health. Ozone is not a primary pollutant, meaning that it is not emitted directly from any source, but is formed by photolytic (that is, activated by sunlight) dissociation of oxygen in other gases, so its concentration is elevated by the presence of other pollutants such as NOx.

Research undertaken subsequent to the publication of the 1988 report by Tyson et al. has found atmospheric dispersion patterns different to those originally expected. Firstly, emissions from high level stacks were found to be deposited to the ground (by downward air flows) at distances relatively close to the emissions sources – in other words, the previous assumption about long-range transport of pollutants emitted into the upper atmosphere by tall chimneys may not be correct (Annegarn: 22). This means that the highest pollution impacts would be encountered within a radius of tens rather than hundreds of kilometres from emissions sources. Second, and consistent with the above point, there was found to be a decreasing concentration of gaseous pollutants, such as sulphur dioxide, as the distance from the high density emission area in the Mpumalanga Highveld increased. Thirdly, the work reported by Annegarn confirmed that power stations give rise to high peak concentrations relatively close to the power stations (16), but that other low-level sources, such as smouldering coal dumps and underground fires in abandoned coal mines, are significant determinants of overall pollution levels.

To summarise then, the data from Eskom suggests that the pollutants which exceed or approach health guidelines most frequently in the Mpumalanga Highveld, are ozone and sulphur dioxide. Of less concern are concentrations of particulates and nitrogen oxides, which are reported to be well within Department of Health guidelines. It should be noted, however, that gaseous and particulate pollutants do not act in isolation, and the combined effect of two or more pollutants can be more significant than the sum of their individual effects.

*Dose-response functions for air pollutants*
The dose-response relationship provides the link between ambient pollution exposures and health outcomes – in this case, respiratory illnesses. The human health effects of pollution exposures have been widely studied in a variety of countries in response to a range of environmental conditions. In South Africa, there have been relatively few studies of the health effects of air pollution, and although a handful of studies have attempted to find correlations between environmental quality – mainly particulate concentrations – and health outcomes – mainly respiratory illnesses – (see for example, Terblanche et al. 1992, 1993)

there have been no studies which have quantified the dose-response function for pollution exposures. [7] It is nonetheless worth highlighting a few salient points emerging from the literature on health effects of air pollution in South Africa.

First, infant mortality data shows that acute respiratory infections (ARI, for example, pneumonia) are the second most common cause of death in South African children, after gastro-related illnesses (Von Schirnding et al. 1991: 81). In Cape Town, ARI ranks as the single greatest cause of infant mortality, along with diarrhoea. The same study reported that the infant mortality rate attributable to ARI in South Africa exceeded that in Western European countries by a factor of 7 to 270.

Second, there is a high probability that large numbers of people are exposed to hazardous levels of air pollution arising mainly from their reliance on coal and wood for their domestic energy needs, but also from other sources of pollution (industrial, vehicular and background dust). Studies of households using coal and wood have found that they face significantly higher risks of respiratory illnesses than those using electricity or other fuels (Terblanche et al. 1992; 1993). However, these studies have not calculated a correlation between pollution exposures and health outcomes – partly because of the complexities raised by the existence of numerous confounding factors (such as tobacco smoke and poor nutritional status).

It is therefore necessary to draw on the international literature to identify dose-response functions which might be applicable to South Africa. For purposes of the project in New York state, USA, which developed the EXMOD model being employed in this study, extensive reviews were undertaken of epidemiological and bio-medical literature, in order to derive dose-response functions which could be used with a satisfactory degree of certainty (Rowe et al. 1994: chapter V). A strict set of criteria were applied in the selection of epidemiological studies for that purpose.[8] On the basis of a large number of studies which followed similar methodologies and were reasonably comparable, dose-response functions were calculated for a range of air pollutants. Sulphates and other gaseous pollutants often constitute a significant portion of particulate matter; since there was found to be no consistent evidence that they were less or more hazardous than other types of airborne particles, they were treated in the same way as other particulates (without double counting them where there were estimates of both sulphates and particulates) (chapter V-4).

The relevant dose-response relationships for particulate matter with a diameter of ten microns or less are summarised in Table 4.6. To accommodate uncertainty in the quantification exercise, low, central and high estimates were

---

7    See Van Horen (1994) or Lerer (1995) for a review and analysis of South African and international studies at the energy-health interface.

8    These are described in detail in Rowe et al. ( V-3 to V-4).

used, with probabilities attached to each. Although the New York study also evaluated and selected dose-response functions for other pollutants, such as lead and air toxics, there is insufficient data in South Africa to permit their quantification – these are classified as Class Three impacts for the present study.

| Health outcome | Pop'n sector | Risk factors | Probability (%) |
|---|---|---|---|
| **Mortality** <br> Daily mortality risk factors given a 1 $\mu$gm$^{-3}$ change in PM10 concentrations | >= 65 years | L 10.1 x 10$^{-8}$ <br> C 16.1 x 10$^{-8}$ <br> H 25.4 x 10$^{-8}$ | L 33 <br> C 34 <br> H 33 |
| | < 65 years | L 0.14 x 10$^{-8}$ <br> C 0.23 x 10$^{-8}$ <br> H 0.35 x 10$^{-8}$ | L 33 <br> C 34 <br> H 33 |
| **Morbidity** <br> Chronic bronchitis annual risk factors given a 1 $\mu$gm$^{-3}$ change in annual PM10 concentrations | >= 25 years | L 3.0 x 10$^{-5}$ <br> C 6.1 x 10$^{-5}$ <br> H 9.3 x 10$^{-5}$ | L 25 <br> C 50 <br> H 25 |
| Respiratory hospital admissions daily risk factors given a 1 $\mu$gm$^{-3}$ change in PM10 concentrations | All | L 1.8 x 10$^{-8}$ <br> C 3.3 x 10$^{-8}$ <br> H 4.8 x 10$^{-8}$ | L 25 <br> C 50 <br> H 25 |
| Emergency room visits daily risk factors given a $\mu$gm$^{-3}$ change in PM10 concentrations | All | L 3.2 x 10$^{-7}$ <br> C 6.5 x 10$^{-7}$ <br> H 9.7 x 10$^{-7}$ | L 25 <br> C 50 <br> H 25 |
| Asthma attacks (AA) daily risk factors given a 1 $\mu$gm$^{-3}$ change in PM10 concentrations For population with asthma | For pop. with asthma | L 0.9 x 10$^{-4}$ <br> C 1.6 x 10$^{-4}$ <br> H 5.4 x 10$^{-4}$ | L 33 <br> C 50 <br> H 17 |
| Restricted activity days risk factors given a 1 $\mu$gm$^{-3}$ change in PM10 concentrations | >= 18 years | L 0.8 x 10$^{-4}$ <br> C 1.6 x 10$^{-4}$ <br> H 2.5 x 10$^{-4}$ | L 33 <br> C 34 <br> H 33 |
| Days with acute respiratory symptoms risk factors given a 1 $\mu$gm$^{-3}$ change in PM10 concentrations | All | L 2.2 x 10$^{-4}$ <br> C 4.6 x 10$^{-4}$ <br> H 7.0 x 10$^{-4}$ | L 25 <br> C 50 <br> H 25 |
| Children with bronchitis annual risk factors given a 1 $\mu$gm$^{-3}$ change in annual PM10 concentrations | <18 years | L 0.8 x 10$^{-3}$ <br> C 1.6 x 10$^{-3}$ <br> H 2.4 x 10$^{-3}$ | L 25 <br> C 50 <br> H 25 |

\* As discussed below, these probabilities have been adjusted to 33: 34: 33 for this study, to reflect the uncertainty inherent in applying US dose-response functions to South Africa.

**Table 4.6** Summary of dose-response relationships for particulates (PM10) in various US studies
*(Rowe et al. 1994: V-38)*

The dose-response relationships given in Table 4.7, for ozone pollution, can be interpreted as follows: for instance in the case of daily mortality risk factors, the central estimate is that one person in $3.3 \times 10^{-6}$, will die for every 1 $\mu gm^{-3}$ increase in ozone concentrations. Put differently, if 40 million South Africans are exposed to an additional 1 $\mu gm^{-3}$ of ozone pollution, then the central estimate implied by this risk factor is that twelve people will die prematurely each year. The low estimate is zero deaths and the high estimate is 24 premature deaths per annum. The probabilities assigned to the low, central and high estimates reflect the degree of confidence in the epidemiological data from which the risk factors were drawn.

In the same way as dose-response relationships were reviewed and selected for particulates, this was also done for health effects arising from ozone pollution. The results of this assessment are summarised in Table 4.7.

| Health outcome | Population sector | Risk factors | Probability* (%) |
|---|---|---|---|
| **Mortality** Daily mortality risk factors given a 1 ppm change in $O_3$ concentrations | All | L 0 C $3.3 \times 10^{-6}$ H $6.6 \times 10^{-6}$ | L 33 C 34 H 33 |
| **Morbidity** Respiratory hospital admissions (RHA) daily risk factors given a 1 ppm change in daily high-hour $O_3$ concentrations | All | L $8.4 \times 10^{-6}$ C $13.7 \times 10^{-6}$ H $19.0 \times 10^{-6}$ | L 33 C 34 H 33 |
| Asthma attacks (AA) daily risk factors given a 1 ppm change in daily high-hour $O_3$ concentrations | For pop. with asthma | L 0.106 C 0.188 H 0.520 | L 33 C 50 H 17 |
| Minor restricted activity days annual individual risk factors given a 1 ppm change in daily high-hour $O_3$ concentrations | All | L $1.93 \times 10^{-2}$ C $4.67 \times 10^{-2}$ H $7.40 \times 10^{-2}$ | L 25 C 50 H 25 |
| Acute respiratory symptoms annual individual risk factors given a 1 ppm change in daily high-hour $O_3$ concentrations | All | L 0.070 C 0.137 H 0.204 | L 25 C 50 H 25 |

* As discussed below, these probabilities have been adjusted to 33: 34: 33 for this study, to reflect the uncertainty inherent in applying US dose-response functions to South Africa.

**Table 4.7** Summary of dose-response relationships for ozone ($O_3$) in various US studies *(Rowe et al. 1994: VI-28)*

The data presented in this way can serve at least two purposes in the present study: first, it can be used in performing valuations of damage costs, by applying economic values to premature deaths. This is commonly done in externality studies. However, this valuation of human life is highly controversial because of the ethical and equity issues which are implicit in such exercises – which is where the second application of this data is useful. It is possible to base policy decisions (for example, in assessing whether pollution abatement technology is warranted), not on the economic costs and benefits – as implied in the first option above – but on objective-led criteria aimed at reducing the physical impacts. For example, the policy objective might be to reduce the mortality rate by 50%, and then the cost-effectiveness of various technological options can be analysed. This can therefore avoid the controversial step of placing economic values on human life (or, more accurately, premature death).

There are two final considerations regarding this dose-response relationship data, the first of which concerns its applicability to South Africa. The population characteristics in the United States and Canada, from where the epidemiological data was derived, differ considerably from those in South Africa, as do environmental conditions. As a result there is an unavoidable degree of uncertainty in applying the data in South Africa. The direction of the bias which may arise, however, (that is, whether the actual health impacts will be under- or over-stated) is not clear. At the most basic level, human physiology and responses to environmental conditions do not differ according to national boundaries. However, there are marked differences in the health status of populations and in average air quality conditions in the two sets of population. The relatively lower level of income and wealth in South Africa, coupled with the higher proportion of people living in conditions of poverty or near-poverty, translates into generally poorer health status. Factors such as lower nutritional status, for instance, mean that South Africans may have lower resistance to environmental hazards and therefore be more susceptible to illness (Terblanche 1995). The bias which this factor introduces means that the above dose-response relationships would tend to understate the actual health outcomes in South Africa.

This is only one of many differences, however, which could introduce bias in either direction. Consequently, in order to account for the additional uncertainty arising from the use of North American dose-response functions in this study, the probability factors in Tables 4.6 and 4.7 will be adjusted to reflect this uncertainty. The probabilities assigned to low, central and high estimates will be adjusted (where this is not already the case) to a 33: 34: 33 distribution, for purposes of the modelling described in the next chapter.

The final factor for present purposes concerns the question of thresholds – the pollution level at which health effects begin to occur. Most environmental regulatory regimes, such as the South African system of guidelines or the

American system of standards, are based on an assumption that there are specific levels of pollution below which threats to public health will be negligible. However, available epidemiological evidence suggests that there may not be such a threshold level for pollutants such as particulates and ozone (Rowe et al.: V-7). Rather, it has been found that health effects occur even below current health guidelines, and in some studies, the dose-response function has been the same for the lowest quartile of particulate pollution as for the highest quartile (V-8). In any event, average levels of air quality in the most densely-populated parts of South Africa are relatively high, so that if there was some threshold in South Africa, it can safely be assumed that this threshold would be exceeded. Thus the default assumptions from the New York study, of a zero threshold, are not adjusted for present purposes.[9]

To conclude, although this is a complex issue with high data requirements, there appears to be sufficient information to use the modelling tools which are available, to attempt a quantification of economic impacts of these health effects. They are therefore given a Class One classification for purposes of this study. The following chapter will proceed with the valuation exercise.

## Air pollution from power generation: impacts of acidic deposition

Pollutants emitted into the atmosphere can have a significant impact on ground-level objects, since they are eventually deposited to the surface, through processes of wet and dry deposition (Piketh & Annegarn 1994). Experience in Europe in the 1970s and 1980s showed that emissions of sulphur dioxide from sources in highly-industrialised areas, such as the Ruhr valley in Germany, or from the coal power stations in the UK, caused high levels of acidic deposition in neighbouring areas (Levy 1995: 59). In the case of Britain's power stations, emissions were transported over long distances and deposited in Norway and Sweden, causing measurable damage to their forests and water courses. Such issues have granted the issue of acidic deposition (or, in popular terms, 'acid rain') a relatively high profile amongst environmental concerns, both internationally and to an extent in South Africa. The view is fairly frequently expressed in South Africa that Eskom's power stations emit large quantities of pollutants which, in turn, cause acid rain (see, for example, Coetzee & Cooper 1991: 132). In scientific circles, the potential risks were first raised in a 1988 report on air pollution in the (then) Eastern Transvaal Highveld, in which the concern

---

9    A more technical question concerns the shape of the dose-response function, particularly at higher levels of pollution: if there are (proportionately) diminishing or increasing human responses at high levels of pollution, this would require a more complex, non-linear function, coupled with data on current ambient pollution levels. Since there is little data available on this question, it can only be flagged here, and so a linear dose-response function is assumed.

was raised that the high concentration of power stations and other sources of anthropogenic pollution, coupled with unfavourable atmospheric conditions, could lead to high levels of acidic deposition (Tyson et al. 1988). This, it was postulated, could cause damage to forests, crops, buildings, fences and other materials sensitive to acidic corrosion.

Following the publication of that report, there have been a number of studies which have measured acidity and have monitored the response of environmental elements such as forest productivity, soil and water chemistry (Olbrich & Kruger 1990; Turner et al. 1990; Turner 1994a).[10] The energy sector of the Southern African Development Community (SADC) even commissioned a study to establish whether emissions from South Africa were causing high levels of acidic deposition in neighbouring states such as Mozambique and Swaziland (Sivertsen et al. 1994). In general, the results of these scientific studies have not yet confirmed the popular notion that 'acid rain' is a serious problem in Mpumalanga province and surrounding regions.

The phenomenon of acidic deposition and its impacts is fairly complex, and is dependent upon a range of local conditions, many of which differ markedly between South Africa and other parts of the world where acidification has been found to be a problem. In order for external costs of acidic deposition to be quantified, several factors need to be considered:

- First, wet deposition rates need to be assessed. This refers to the quantity of acidifying species (such as sulphates) washed out of the atmosphere during rainfall episodes. Tyson et al. (1988: 62) reported rates of up to, and sometimes in excess of 20 kg/ha per annum, which is regarded as a critical threshold in other contexts. Monitoring by Eskom, however, found 'reasonably low' levels of wet deposition over a seven year period (Turner 1993 in Piketh & Annegarn 1994: 5).

- Second, dry deposition rates should also be estimated. Since South Africa is a relatively dry country, it has been suggested that dry deposition of acidic species (that is, not through rain or mist) could be even more significant than elsewhere (Tyson et al. 1988: 65). Eskom's early calculations suggested that dry deposition could exceed wet deposition by a factor of four in some regions on the Highveld, with dry rates of around 20 kg/ha per year (Turner 1994b: 6). Similarly, Olbrich and du Toit (1993) found that dry deposition rates exceeded wet deposition rates by 2.7 times. In one study which calculated dry deposition rates at two sites (one on the Mpumalanga escarpment and the other in the Lowveld), dry deposition rates were found to be fairly low, at 5.3 and 1.2 kg/ha/year respectively (Piketh & Annegarn: 4). In another study, by contrast, sulphate deposition rates were estimated

---

10   For a review of these studies up to 1993, see Van Horen (1994: 11).

to range from 49 to 81 kg/h per year (Wells 1993, cited in Piketh & Annegarn). There appears, therefore, to be a wide range of estimates of actual deposition rates at various locations.

- An important factor in assessing damages from acidification, is the sensitivity of soils and ground cover. Soils in the Mpumalanga province have varying degrees of sensitivity, and are often fairly alkaline, in which cases acidic deposition can initially have a positive effect on the productivity of soils, crops and forests. Efforts have recently been made by the CSIR to develop an information system which contains information on the sensitivity of soils and water systems in the Mpumalanga province, against which deposition data can be plotted, so that areas of greatest concern can be targeted (Olbrich et al. 1995). A range of maps can be produced using this system, showing the sensitivity of soils, water, actual deposition rates, and combinations of any of these. This system, known as the Atmospheric Deposition Risk Advisory System (ADRAS) could be used as a tool in identifying areas where damages will be most significant, and undertaking appropriate ameliorative measures.

- One further dimension of acidic deposition relates to the corrosion of buildings, vehicles, fences and other susceptible materials. Apart from anecdotal observations that this represents a significant problem in some regions, monitoring by Eskom of corrosion rates at various sites in Mpumalanga and the Vaal Triangle suggests that rates are low, although limitations on the monitoring techniques were acknowledged (Van Rensburg 1994). Quantitative information on this impact is therefore scarce.

Only one field study has been undertaken to-date in the Mpumalanga Highveld with a view to assessing whether any damage has occurred to commercial forest plantations (Olbrich & Kruger 1990). Very small changes were observed in that study, although evidence was not conclusive; it was reported that commercial forests did not appear to have suffered any substantial ill-effects from acidic deposition. International experience suggests that a critical threshold may exist, up to which few if any damages are observed, and beyond which more extensive crop and forest damage may occur (Scholes 1995). On this basis, therefore, it appears prudent to follow the ADRAS approach which could highlight high-risk areas and monitor forest productivity to ensure that damages do not occur. Given that the Mpumalanga Highveld is an important location for commercial forestry in South Africa, any damages which result from acidification, could have significant economic effects. For the present, however, the state of information means that this impact has to be classified as a Class Two impact.

## Air pollution from power generation: visibility impacts

Reduced visibility is one result of air pollution which attracts considerable public comment and criticism. It requires no scientific or technical expertise to observe 'dirty' air, hence there is frequent comment in the press and popular literature regarding hazy atmospheric conditions (see for example Clarke (1991)). Reduced visibility is a phenomenon which occurs fairly widely, both in cities – notably Cape Town, which has a reasonably serious brown haze problem (De Villiers & Dutkiewicz) – and in rural areas. As with other forms of air quality monitoring, there is no systematic monitoring of visibility conditions by an independent authority acting primarily in the interests of the public. Nor are there any standards or guidelines regarding 'acceptable' levels of visibility reduction. Eskom, partly in response to criticisms directed against itself as a contributor to the poor visibility in the Mpumalanga Highveld, undertook some quantitative analysis of visibility conditions in the region (Turner 1994a). This analysis utilised the results collected in its pollution monitoring network, particularly the Elandsfontein station, located in the centre of the Highveld.

Results from this analysis showed that the mean visibility range for the entire period May 1985 to December 1993 was 76 km, with a seasonal high of about 105 km for January and a low of 60 km for September (Turner: 5, 11). Average results, however, are perhaps not the most meaningful, since aesthetic values are influenced more heavily by poor visibility occurrences than by long-term averages. On this basis, the visibility range fares poorly. Whilst the range was over 100 km on 10% of the days measured – corresponding to low levels of visible pollution – it was as low as 40 km on almost half the days, as low as 30 km on over 20% of the days, as low as 20 km on almost 10% of the days, and less than 10 km on 1.1% of days – that is, 4 days per year (Turner: 5,11).[11] It is perhaps the latter figures which reinforce most strongly the common view that air quality is severely degraded in parts of Mpumalanga province.

Establishing that a visibility problem exists, however, is easier than quantifying the contributing factors. Visibility can be impaired by naturally-occurring phenomena such as high levels of water vapour (which becomes 'mist' at high densities) and natural dust in the atmosphere, as well as by human-induced phenomena. The latter include emissions from industrial activity, household fuels, motor vehicles, vegetation fires, changes in land cover resulting from mining, agriculture, waste production, and so on. To a greater or lesser extent, all of these sources are present in the Mpumalanga Highveld where seven of the nine operational coal power stations are located. Eskom's analysis of the diurnal patterns of visibility conditions, which do not correlate with observed

---

11    By comparison, some US states set the criteria level for 'severe' visibility degradation at 16 km (Turner 1994a: 5).

emissions patterns from its power stations, concludes that emissions of particulates and sulphur dioxide by power stations 'do not play a major role in regional visibility impairment' (Turner: 6). Rather, Eskom attributes poor visibility mainly to 'low level and regional sources' which include smoke from biomass burning, smouldering coal dumps and surface dust. Interestingly, Eskom's results show that the visibility range improved by about 5% per year at its Elandsfontein site from 1985 to 1993, and this was attributed to the improved control of smouldering coal dumps, the closure of old power stations with lower chimney stacks, and the effect of drought on biomass burning and surface dust (insofar as the latter affect rainfall chemistry).

The relatively high degree of uncertainty, coupled with the non-transferability of experience from elsewhere, means that visibility impacts fall into the Class Two category for purposes of this study.

### Water quality impacts from power generation

Power stations are important agents in the non-agricultural water sector in South Africa. Not only are they a significant consumptive user of water, but they also return significant quantities of water back to the environment. Over time Eskom's water policy has changed: in response to increasing scarcity, two of its newer power stations employ dry cooling towers which reduce the net quantity of water consumed. In addition, it has adopted stricter policies regarding the quality of water it returns to the environment. Eskom (1995b: 20) reports that it strives towards a 'zero effluent' water policy, which means that the quality of the water it returns to rivers and dams must be at least as good as the water it draws from those sources. Thus water used in the thermal fuel cycle is recycled up to the point where it is too polluted, after which it is used for less demanding purposes. For example, water which is eventually no longer being used in the fuel cycle, is used on the ash dumps to reduce the amount of ash blown into the atmosphere. In 1994, Eskom (20) reported that about 8% (17 083 megalitres) of the water it consumed was released to public streams and, of this, ten megalitres did not conform to quality standards set by the Department of Water Affairs and Forestry . This is a fraction of one per cent of its water emissions.

This is not to say, however, that the coal power stations have no impact on water quality at all. Firstly, the upstream impacts of coal mining on water quality have already been noted in an earlier section. Secondly, problems sometimes arise in the implementation of the zero effluent policy, such as where leakages occur, as described above, or during periods of high rainfall where storage dams cannot accomodate increased flow volumes. In 1994, six such incidents were reported at Eskom's power stations, and although permission was obtained for these releases from DWAF (Eskom: 20), their economic costs could feasibly have been non-zero.

A third impact which arises in some cases, is positive. The power stations require water of reasonably good quality, otherwise the rates of corrosion and weathering of plant and equipment are unacceptably high, and consequently, at some power stations, water has to purified before use in the power stations. Even after that water has been through the fuel cycle and it is returned to the receiving water body, it can be of higher quality than when it was withdrawn (Fedorsky 1995). Insofar as there is no compensation or rebate accruing to Eskom in respect of this improvement, a positive externality arises.

The valuation of water quality impacts is complex, although not impossible. The general approach would be to impute a shadow price for water which is no longer usable; this price would reflect the opportunity cost of rendering that volume of water unusable – based on the marginal cost of obtaining water of adequate quality from an alternative source. A second valuation approach which could be used would be to quantify the expenditure incurred by downstream users in returning that water to an adequate quality – so-called 'defensive expenditure'. In some cases, valuation of water quality changes also include changes in the productivity of commercial fishing or recreational fishing markets. For example, in the New York state study, water quality impacts could include negative impacts on recreational and commercial activities in the Hudson River, as well as the Great Lakes which lie to the north of the state (Rowe et al.: XVI-2). In South Africa, on the other hand, these do not represent significant activities in the proximity of power stations; the impacts of other water consumption sectors, most notably agriculture, dominate issues of water quality.

On balance, this category of environmental impacts is not considered to represent a significant external effect (either negative or positive) for South Africa's power stations. It is thus given Class Three status for purposes of this study. Of greater relevance in relation to power generation's impact on water resources, are the impacts of coal mining on water quality, and the pricing of water consumption in once-through power stations, both of which have been addressed in previous sections of this chapter.

### Greenhouse gas emissions from power generation

Electricity generation, where it is based on coal-power, is unavoidably a significant source of greenhouse gas (GHG) emissions.[13] The principal GHGs

---

13   Briefly, GHGs are relevant insofar as they are widely believed to enhance the naturally-occurring greenhouse effect – in terms of which GHGs increase the ability of the earth's atmosphere to retain warmth. The balance of scientific opinion suggests that continued emission of GHGs at present rates will lead to global climate change, with variable, but often negative consequences in many regions of the world. For more details on recent developments in the international climate change debate, see Rowlands (1995a), and on the South African energy sector's contribution, see Van Horen & Simmonds (1995).

are carbon dioxide ($CO_2$), methane, chlorofluorocarbons and nitrous oxides, the first two of which are most significant in South Africa. South Africa was responsible for about 1.2% of global GHG emissions in 1988, making it the eighteenth largest source in the world, and one of largest sources on a per capita basis (Van Horen & Simmonds 1995). It was also the largest source of GHGs in Africa, accounting for 15% of the continent's $CO_2$ emissions.

Significant quantities of carbon dioxide are emitted by the electricity generation sector, and smaller amounts of methane during coal mining. Eskom is the single largest source of GHGs in South Africa, which, by its calculations, amounted to some 142.9 million tons of carbon dioxide in 1994 (Eskom 1995b). The emissions by each of the coal power stations is shown in Table 4.8.

|  | Total $CO_2$ emissions (million tons) |
| --- | --- |
| Arnot | 4.5 |
| Duvha | 20.6 |
| Hendrina | 12.7 |
| Kendal | 17.8 |
| Kriel | 14.3 |
| Lethabo | 18.2 |
| Matimba | 20.0 |
| Matla | 18.2 |
| Tutuka | 16.6 |
| Total | 142.9 |

**Table 4.8** Carbon dioxide emissions from Eskom's power stations in 1994
*(Source: Eskom Generation group)*

In addition to emissions of carbon dioxide, the power sector is also responsible for a portion of methane emissions emanating from the coal mining sector – notably underground mines. For present purposes, however, these will not be quantified: although the global warming potential of methane far exceeds that of carbon dioxide, most policy attention and quantification exercises to-date have focused on reducing carbon emissions. Moreover, less than half of Eskom's coal is sourced from underground mines which emit most of the methane. The exclusion of methane emissions has the effect, therefore, of understating the potential damages attributable to electricity generation in South Africa.

There is a vast body of international literature which has sprung up around the climate change phenomenon, addressing both its physical and political-economic dimensions. It is impossible to summarise here all aspects of this issue;

instead, a few salient points will be made in relation to the impacts of climate change on South Africa's electricity generation industry. Firstly, South Africa is unlikely to be faced with any binding commitments to reduce its emissions of GHGs in the near future. As a 'developing country' – defined in terms of the Framework Convention on Climate Change (FCCC) – South Africa will not face the same targets for GHG reductions as the industrialised countries.[13] At present, the latter's targets are limited to the stabilisation of GHG emissions at 1990 levels by the year 2000 (FCCC, Articles 4.2 (a) and (b)).

A second pertinent factor follows from the first: although the country will not have any immediate onerous obligations upon ratification, it is not improbable that it could face some intermediate targets further down the road, if differentiation is made within the 'developing country' category, by virtue of its relatively high level of income and emissions (Rowlands 1995b). Thus, it is important that South African policy-making takes explicit account of the climate change issue, and adopts a proactive stance in international negotiations.

Thirdly, there is considerable uncertainty around the climate change issue in various of its dimensions. Clearly, this uncertainty serves the interests of many groups and nations (for example, the oil-producing countries); so it is important to establish the boundaries of this uncertainty. One of the key uncertainties at present is around the potential impacts of climate change on specific sub-regions, such as Southern Africa. This uncertainty, exacerbated by the extremely long time periods over which it might occur,[14] makes it extremely difficult to make assessments of the economic and social costs of possible climate change, which may include, for example, the costs of possible increased drought in the future, and more frequent occurrences of extreme weather events (storms, floods, droughts). Several attempts have been made internationally to estimate the range of damage costs which might result from climate change (for example, Cline 1992; Fankhauser 1992; Nordhaus 1993); not surprisingly, these have produced very different estimates and have attracted their share of criticism. This uncertainty presents special difficulties for the present study.

What is much more certain, however, is that the climate change issue will not disappear from the international political economy in the near future. Given the prominent role of South Africa amongst developing countries, it is essential that the issue is not ignored. Although there is considerable uncertainty surrounding possible scenarios of damages, enough work has been done internationally to permit some quantification – provided the level of uncertainty is taken into account explicitly – hence this impact is assigned to the Class One

---

13   The future tense is used because, as at the end of 1995, South Africa had signed but not yet ratified the FCCC.

14   With concomitant importance attached to the selection of a discount rate when economic effects are being considered.

category. The next chapter presents a range of estimates of the damage costs which might be attributable to emissions of greenhouse gases, which collectively allow for analysis of the range of implications which may emerge from international political negotiations in the coming decade or more.

## Externalities in South Africa's nuclear fuel cycle

The nuclear fuel cycle internationally has been the subject of considerable analysis in the last two decades or more, particularly in relation to the environmental and other externalities with which it is associated. Many of the environmental impacts in the nuclear industry can be characterised as having relatively low probability but high (or potentially catastrophic) impact if they do occur. Thus externality studies have usually focused on the risk of such impacts, and on society's valuation of those risks (rather than valuation of the impacts themselves).

In addition to the externalities associated with potential catastrophic accidents, there are two other kinds of externalities of relevance. The first relates to those environmental impacts which occur regularly and are not fully internalised into the price of nuclear electricity – occupational health hazards, air or water pollution, and so on. These can be treated in essentially the same way as impacts arising from the coal fuel cycle. Another kind of externality may be termed a 'fiscal externality' – in other words, a fiscal transfer payment (for example, a subsidy) which is made to the nuclear industry, and which is not reflected in the price of nuclear electricity (Lockwood 1992). Whilst this is not an environmental externality per se, it is a potentially material externality in South Africa, which could be significant in relation to the price of electricity, and so it is included in the scope of this study.

### Environmental impacts and risks in the nuclear fuel cycle

Several actual or potential environmental impacts of significance occur in South Africa's nuclear sector:

● The risk of catastrophic accidents (on the scale of Chernobyl) cannot be ruled out completely, although it is reduced by the existence of a strict safety regime governing all stages of the nuclear industry in South Africa. Externalities studies elsewhere, in attempts to quantify these risks in economic terms, have focused on society's valuation of those risks (Krupnick et al. 1993). In South Africa, there has been no such analysis to-date, which does not make this quantification exercise feasible for present purposes. However, the fact that Koeberg power station is located about 50 kilometres from the Cape Town metropolitan area, which has a population of over two million, means that the impact of any accident, should one occur, would probably be very large.

- International experience with the costs of decommissioning nuclear power facilities is that they are greater than anticipated, mainly because of higher safety and environmental standards than were foreseen at the time of construction (MacKerron 1992). This means that costs have to be incurred in the future which have not been accounted (provided) for in the current pricing structure of nuclear electricity. The same could hold true for South Africa's nuclear industry, although the absence of any public information about this makes any assessment in this regard necessarily speculative.

- Nuclear power generation produces a number of radioactive waste products, which are typically categorised according to their degree of radioactivity. Low-level wastes are stored at the Vaalputs site in the Northern Cape province under high standards of safety, and thus their costs are essentially internalised. However, the storage and disposal of high-level radioactive wastes remain problematic (as is the case internationally) and, in the interim, these wastes are stored on site at Koeberg power station (Auf der Heyde 1993). Given the extremely long time periods for which high-level wastes remain hazardous – thousands of years – the potential environmental and health costs associated with future accidents are, simultaneously, highly uncertain, potentially large, and long-lasting. Their valuation thus presents significant difficulties, not least because so much is dependant upon the choice of a discount rate.

- The operation of a nuclear power station is associated with any number of small incidents and procedural breakdowns which, because of the nature of the nuclear generation process, means that workers are exposed to potentially serious occupational risks. Although difficult to quantify, these risks are not accounted for in wage rates (as in the case of coal mining) which means the risks are not internalised. This is not to deny that the nuclear industry employs stringent health and safety standards for its workers; nonetheless, the reality is that workers are exposed to potentially significant risks by virtue of the nature of the process, and are not compensated for this. At the ANC's nuclear conference held in February 1994, worker representatives highlighted the health and safety hazards to which they were exposed – notwithstanding safety procedures.

- Finally, to the extent that links existed between civilian nuclear power and military nuclear weaponry – links which were partly confirmed by the admission of former President de Klerk in 1993 that the apartheid government possessed at least six nuclear weapons – they constitute a category of externalities which are highly uncertain, but so large as to be of significance. Clearly, were any such weapons to be utilised (although it is difficult to imagine where or how these might have been deployed) the costs could have been enormous.

These external environmental effects, both current and future, existing and potential, are of significance in aggregate, but present considerable difficulties for any economic analysis. Insufficient data exists in the South African context to quantify society's valuation of the risks with which these impacts are associated. This data scarcity has not been helped by the pervasive secrecy which has surrounded (and continues to surround) the industry. Furthermore, given the limited resources available for this project, these externalities will not be further assessed, save to note that they are potentially highly significant, and are therefore assigned to the Class Two impact category.

## Fiscal externalities in the nuclear industry

A final category of externalities which arises in the South African electricity generation industry is those subsidies which have flowed to the nuclear industry since the beginning of the 1970s. This fiscal externality is significant in relation to the amount of electricity which has been produced. Unlike the coal-fired electricity sector, which has historically received little or no financial subsidy from public funds, the local nuclear industry has enjoyed a very privileged position in this respect. This is similar to the nuclear industry in the UK and elsewhere (Lockwood 1992).

The nuclear industry has received the lion's share of the Department of Mineral and Energy Affairs (DMEA) annual parliamentary grant since 1971/72. Table 4.9 shows the average annual allocation to the nuclear industry: the Atomic Energy Corporation (AEC, or its predecessor, the Atomic Energy Board), the former Nuclear Development Corporation (Nucor) and the Council for Nuclear Safety (CNS), for the period 1971/72 to 1995/96. It is evident from the table that considerable resources have been directed to the local nuclear industry; these have been directed to three main categories of expenditure: capital expenditure, operating expenditure and servicing and repayment of loans (Auf der Heyde 1993: 7). Arguably, not all of these amounts should be attributed to the nuclear generation industry, since non-electricity aspects of the industry have also benefited from state subsidies: notably the nuclear bomb programme, research and development in non-electric areas, and the production of medical isotopes. Unfortunately there is no publicly available information on the allocation of the subsidy to these various sectors; consequently, calculations and assumptions have to be made on the basis of the information available.

| Period | Annual average (Nominal Rm) | % of DMEA budget | Annual average (1995 Rm) |
|---|---|---|---|
| 1971/72 to 1975/76 | 21.2 | 32.0 | 250.6 |
| 1976/77 to 1980/81 | 110.7 | 40.8 | 740.7 |
| 1981/82 to 1985/86 | 363.0 | 70.3 | 1 336.5 |
| 1986/87 to 1990/91 | 686.2 | 79.7 | 1 403.5 |
| 1991/92 to 1995/96 | 524.5 | 70.3 | 619.3 |
| Total 1971/72 to 1995/96 | 8 528.0 | 69.3 | 21753.3 |

* Nominal Rands adjusted to real 1995 Rands by Production Price Index, using CSS (1995).

**Table 4.9**  Subsidies to the nuclear industry in nominal and real
terms, 1971/72 to 1995/96
*(calculated from Auf der Heyde 1993; CSS 1995)*

To be conservative, only those costs which are known to be related to electricity generation will be included in this analysis; thus these represent a minimum estimate of the fiscal subsidy to the industry, and probably underestimate the actual costs. On the operating expenditure side, the relevant costs include those of conversion, enrichment, fabrication, decommissioning and waste disposal: according to Auf der Heyde (1993: 25), these totalled R3 062 million (1995 Rands) for the 9 fiscal years from 1987/88 to 1995/96, which represents 46% of total operating expenditure, or 37% of total nuclear funding (calculated from Auf der Heyde (5,7)).

With regard to capital expenditure, the costs of the conversion, enrichment and fabrication plants (but not the 'Y-plant') are assumed to relate to electricity generation; these allocations amounted to R2 686 million in 1995 Rands, or 62% of the total capital expenditure reported in Auf der Heyde (24). Correspondingly, it is assumed that the same proportion (62%) of finance charges is attributable to the electricity component of the subsidy; this amounts to R1 620 million (in 1995 Rands) for the nine years to 1995/96.

The total of these allocations for the nine year period 1987/88 to 1995/96 is R7 368 million, in 1995 Rands. A portion of the nuclear allocation prior to 1987/88 should also be apportioned to the nuclear electricity sector, but since this information is not publicly available, further assumptions are required. It will be assumed (conservatively) that all relevant capital expenditure is included in the above estimate (and likewise for corresponding finance charges); for operating expenditure, it will be assumed that the percentage of total nuclear funding attributable to the electricity sector, was the same as after 1987/88: that is, 37% of the total. This yields an estimate of R4 876 million in 1995

Rands (calculated from Auf der Heyde (5). To this should be added the allocation to the Council for Nuclear Safety (CNS), which also represents an external cost of operating a nuclear power facility: this amounted to R54 million in 1995 Rands, for the period 1983/84 to 1995/96.

To summarise then, the total public allocation to the nuclear industry, for purposes of electricity generation, is estimated to be R12 298 million (in 1995 Rands) for the period 1971/72 to 1995/96. This represents 57% of the total government subsidy of the nuclear industry for that period, and can be taken as a minimum estimate, in the absence of public disclosure of this information.

This subsidy has not been internalised into the price of nuclear electricity – the effects of doing so are described in the next chapter. Given that there is sufficient data at this aggregated level to quantify the extent of the fiscal externality, it is accorded a Class One ranking.

## Summary of external effects

Thus far, a range of potentially significant external effects in the South African coal and nuclear fuel cycles have been described, in terms of their scale and frequency. For policy-making purposes this can, in itself, be helpful insofar as policy goals might demand that one or more of these physical impacts be addressed. The data presented in this chapter constitutes something of a baseline, against which the success of otherwise of policies and strategies can be measured. Targets or objectives could be set: for example, a 50% reduction in the rate of worker illness and mortality on coal mines, and economic analysis undertaken to find the most cost-effective ways of achieving that goal. If this is the preferred approach, then it will not be necessary to proceed to the final step in the damage function approach, which is the economic valuation of the physical damages described thus far.

For purposes of this study, however, it is deemed useful to attempt a quantification of the economic value of the external effects in the generation sector. This is of special relevance for South Africa's industrial policy, given the importance being attached to low electricity prices as a basis for economic growth. This quantification will be undertaken in the following chapter, and to this end, the classification of the environmental impacts described thus far, is summarised in Table 4.10.

| | Class One | Class Two | Class Three |
|---|:---:|:---:|:---:|
| *Coal fuel cycle* Coal mining: morbidity & mortality | ✔ | ✔ | |
| Coal mining: air & water pollution | | ✔ | ✔ |
| Generation: water consumption | ✔ | | |
| Generation: air pollution & health impacts | ✔ | ✔ | |
| Generation: air pollution & acidification | | ✔ | |
| Generation: air pollution & visibility | | ✔ | |
| Generation: water quality impacts | | | ✔ |
| Generation: greenhouse gas emissions | ✔ | | |
| Other impacts (EMFs, aesthetics, etc) | | | ✔ |
| *Nuclear fuel cycle* Fiscal subsidy | ✔ | | |
| Other impacts (risk of accident, waste disposal, decommissioning costs, etc) | | ✔ | |

**Table 4.10** Summary of potentially significant environmental impacts and their classification in this study

From Table 4.10 it is evident that five main externalities – those falling into Class One – are quantified in this study. It is worth emphasising again before proceeding, that the omission of certain impacts from this valuation exercise does not necessarily mean that they are insignificant or immaterial in economic terms: rather, it could be the case that insufficient information exists to make any meaningful attempt at quantification.

# 5

# Valuation of externalities in South Africa's electricity sector

The measurement of environmental and resource values enjoys a long tradition in economic theory and practice; it has also received much policy attention in recent decades. Not only is there considerable experience in industrialised countries, however, there is also much uncertainty and scepticism about the practicalities or ethics of valuing environmental elements, especially where these involve human health and quality of life. Whilst environmental valuation is undoubtedly a complex and controversial subject, policy analysis is not well served by ruling out this approach altogether. Rather, a more strategic and critical employment of environmental valuation techniques in appropriate circumstances can serve a useful purpose in developing policy in the industrial, energy and environmental sectors. Consequently, this chapter addresses the final step in the damage function approach: the valuation of those externalities in the coal and nuclear fuel cycles which appear to be significant and about which there is sufficient information to make meaningful estimates of their economic value. Thus the five externalities which were assigned a 'Class One' impact in Chapter Four are considered here:

- morbidity and mortality effects of coal mining;
- full economic pricing of water consumption in power stations;
- morbidity and mortality effects of air pollution from power stations;
- damage costs arising from emission of greenhouse gases;
- fiscal subsidies directed to the production of nuclear electricity.

The analysis which follows aims to produce a range of estimates of the external costs incurred by society in respect of each of these impacts. These external costs will be estimated in monetary terms, and in terms of a cost (in cents) per kWh of electricity generated. The latter is one of the key outputs of this study, as it permits an assessment of the extent to which South Africa's electricity prices reflect external costs. The section which follows briefly outlines the valuation approach used in respect of changes to human morbidity and mortality. Finally, in recognition of the complexities and uncertainties inherent in the valuation exercise, the chapter summarises the main limitations of this study.

# Valuation of morbidity and mortality effects: methodological issues

Before making estimates of the external costs of the five categories of externality identified earlier, it is important to describe briefly the valuation approach which is being adopted in this study in respect of changes in human morbidity and mortality. This is directly relevant to the first and third externalities listed above, and indirectly relevant to the fourth externality.

A number of valuation approaches can be used to value morbidity and mortality. Dealing first with morbidity, two broad methods can be used: first, those based on individual preferences, that is, willingness to pay (WTP) for environmental and health improvements, or willingness to accept compensation (WAC) for deterioration; second, those methods based on resource or opportunity costs (Freeman 1993: 343). In the neo-classical literature, economists generally prefer the individual preference approach because it is consistent with the underlying basis of microeconomic theory, in which utility or welfare is a function of a person's willingness to pay for it. Furthermore, WTP (or WAC) approaches are generally considered more appropriate because they are believed to yield a more complete estimate of a person's valuation of illness: WTP values include, typically, not only the opportunity costs of illness, but also a person's valuation of the discomfort or displeasure from being less than fully healthy. By contrast, it is argued that opportunity cost approaches focus only on the direct costs of illness – such as expenditure on medical care and foregone income from not working – and do not place any value on the more subjective (but very real) discomfort or displeasure experienced whilst being sick, which should probably have a non-zero value (Freeman: 34). Empirical data in the US suggests that WTP usually exceeds the direct cost of illness by a factor of 1.3 to 2.4, depending on the health effect (Rowe et al 1994: X-30).

Individual preference approaches for valuing morbidity are, however, not necessarily the ideal method in a developing country context such as South Africa. There are several reasons for this: firstly, there have been few if any studies in this country of people's WTP or WAC with respect to health effects (or any other environmental element, for that matter). Thus the empirical basis for such estimates is weak. Secondly, even if such information was available, it would be problematic to use it in a context of an extremely unequal distribution of income: all other things equal, the WTP for health improvements of a poor person would be lower than that of a wealthy person. Using such WTP valuations may be consistent with economic efficiency criteria (as embodied in the Pareto criterion), but could have consequences for policy decisions which are extremely inequitable.[1] This issue is more pertinent in a country such as South Africa than it is in North America or Europe, where WTP and WAC measures have been used much more frequently.

Thirdly, WTP and WAC valuation approaches may, in fact, *understate* the value of a health risk – the inverse of the commonly prevailing situation in wealthier countries (as embodied in the ratio of WTP to cost of illness reported above). To illustrate, it could easily happen that society's valuation of a person's health, as expressed for instance in its budgetary allocation to public health care in its hospitals and clinics, exceeds the amount which a person would be willing to expend on medical care – for the simple reason that their income may be insufficient to allow them to pay. Thus, for example, it is possible to foresee a situation in which a cancer patient is unable ('unwilling') to pay for expensive radiotherapy treatment (and would therefore have a low WTP were this to be measured), but where society deems it worth expending the required amount to provide that person with the best treatment. In this context, a valuation approach which is based on WTP might give an assessment of an individual's willingness to pay (determined as it is, by income), which is less than the actual amount expended by society.

Consequently, the valuation approach adopted in this study in respect of morbidity effects is based on the *opportunity cost* approach. Thus the valuation of health effects generally includes actual expenditure on health care (both public and private), transport costs, medication and so on, and foregone income, such as lost time at work. This approach, sometimes also called the 'cost of illness approach', has the added advantage of being less abstract and easier to measure and substantiate. In general, the opportunity cost data used in this study has been derived from health specialists' estimates of typical treatment regimes and costs, and from other primary or secondary sources of information.

Turning to the valuation of premature death, the complexities and controversies are significant. Not least is the ethical problem which arises in reducing human life to a finite monetary value, and the implications this holds for policy-making. The economics literature frequently makes a distinction between the valuation of human life *per se*, and the value individuals or society place on the risk or probability of early mortality (Freeman 1993; Pearce et al 1991: 5).

---

1 For instance, all other things equal, it would be economically efficient – but not necessarily equitable or socially acceptable – to construct a new power station near a poorer residential area rather than a wealthier area, since the latter's valuation of clean air would be higher than the former's.

The argument goes that there is a difference between simply placing a value on human life, and placing a monetary estimate on a person's trade-off between various risks of death. This distinction is somewhat pedantic and does little to counter the general distaste with valuing mortality.

A more compelling justification for placing monetary values on human life is that in many respects, this is done already by individuals and society, implicitly in many of their activities, often without making the trade-offs explicit. This is acutely evident, for example, in the decision over the allocation of public resources to primary health care services versus high-level tertiary care such as heart transplants. Implicit in these allocative decisions is society's (or parts of society's) valuation of lost lives, be they poor rural children, or wealthy urban professionals. Thus to assign some monetary value to human life merely makes transparent or explicit whatever judgements are being made. Furthermore, provided the values are used in a decision-making context which seeks to balance the full range of interests as best as possible, the use of monetary values for early death can serve an important *strategic* purpose: for example, by highlighting the losses suffered by society due to inadequate supplies of potable water and sanitation services, a case can be made, perhaps more strongly, for investment in improved service levels.

The economic valuation of early death should also not be seen or used out of context: the placing of monetary values on death and other environmental elements is used merely as one aid in decision-making, along with a range of other inputs: social, political and ecological. As mentioned earlier, there is no obligation even to use these economic valuations for decisions over the allocation of resources -decisions can be made on the basis of physical or health objectives. Moreover, it is possible to use a range of estimates for the value of premature mortality, to reflect the degree of uncertainty which exists.

This study uses economic valuations of human life in full awareness of the complexities and ethical problems of doing so, but this is done, firstly, in order to maintain methodological consistency with the remainder of the study and, secondly, because this may serve a strategic purpose in this study, by highlighting the high human cost of certain environmental impacts.

As in the case of morbidity effects, there are a number of methods which may be adopted to value premature death. One is sometimes described as the 'human capital' approach: essentially, this entails valuing a lost life at the discounted value of future income which that person might have been expected to generate. Most simply, average GDP would be used as a proxy for that person's income; this was done, for instance, in the study by Dutkiewicz and de Villiers (1993). Problems soon arise, however, particularly if there is any differentiation between social classes, age groups, males and females, employed and unemployed, and so on – the implications of the differing values which result are especially problematic for policy and resource allocation decisions where 'equity' is a goal: in most societies, adult males of about 25 years of age will have the highest 'value' (Freeman: 324). Furthermore, this approach is highly sensitive to the choice of a discount rate: for example, for a male child between one and four years of age in the US in 1987, at a discount rate of 2.5%, its human capital value would have been $761 000, compared to only $60 000 at a discount rate of 10% (Freeman: 325).

The alternative valuation approach used for mortality entails the use of individual preference approaches: not so much a person's willingness to pay to avoid death (which would probably be their entire wealth) or willingness to accept compensation for death (which would probably be an infinite amount), but the valuation of a changed probability of death. Such decisions are made on a daily basis: for example, in paying a higher price for a ticket with an airline or bus service which is considered safer than the alternatives.

The choice of values of premature death for South Africa is made difficult by two factors: first, there have been no studies of this nature in this country from which values can be derived. Secondly, there are sharp inequalities in the distribution of income and wealth, which presents problems (from an equity perspective) if *differential* valuations are used for different income groups – as would apply if the human capital approach was adopted. Taking both of these issues into account, this study uses a consistent valuation set for premature death across the entire population in the region. In other words, no differentiation is made in economic terms between a premature death in Mozambique or Mpumalanga, Sandton or Soweto. The valuation approach adopted in this study for mortality effects will draw on international studies of revealed preference, adjusted for South African conditions. At least two major international exter-nality valuation exercises have undertaken their own reviews of the literature and on that basis, selected a range of values for premature deaths. These estimates, which are based on revealed preference approaches, are shown in Table 5.1. The study by Rowe et al (1994) was undertaken for New York state, USA, and drew upon North American valuation studies; likewise, the study by ETSU (1995) estimated values for the European Union.

Simply applying these valuations to South African conditions would be problematic from a theoretical perspective, since individual valuations of the risk of death must, by definition, take account of income levels. Assuming these valuations vary in direct proportion to income, an adjustment can be made to the North American and European values to reflect average South African income levels. These adjustment factors are also shown in Table 5.1.

|  | USA | European Union | South Africa |
|---|---|---|---|
| GDP per capita ($ 1992) | 23 240<br>*(World Bank 1995: 163)* | 19 678<br>(calculated from World<br>Bank 1995: 163) | 1 680[1] |
| Income adjustment factor | 13.8 | 11.7 | 1 |
| Mortality valuations<br>low estimate<br>central estimate<br>high estimate | *Rowe et al (1994:X-14)*<br>$1 700 000<br>$3 300 000<br>$6 600 000 | *ETSU (1995: 49)*<br>ecu 2 100 000<br>ecu 2 600 000<br>ecu 3 000 000 |  |
| Income-adjusted<br>valuations (1995 R)[2]<br>low estimate<br>central estimate<br>high estimate | <br><br>450 042<br>873 612<br>1 747 224 | <br><br>857 493<br>1 061 659<br>1 224 991 | Average:<br>653 768<br>967 635<br>1 436 107 |

**Notes**
1. Calculated as follows: GDP for 1992 of R238 711 million (SAIRR 1995: 380), divided by population estimate for 1992 of 38.8 million (1994 estimate of 40.7 million, reduced by annual growth rate of 2.44%) (SAIRR: 5).
2. The US and EU valuations are divided by the income adjustment factor to give South African valuations. The following exchange rates are used: $1 = R3.66, ecu 1 = R4.78.

**Table 5.1**  Valuations of premature deaths used in international studies and in this study

The figures in the bottom right cell of Table 5.1 represent the average of the adjusted valuations for the American and European studies in the last row of the table. If these numbers are rounded to the nearest R100 000, the following valuations for premature deaths are derived:

low estimate        R700 000
central estimate    R1 000 000
high estimate       R1 400 000.

These estimates will be used in this study for purposes of attaching an economic value to premature mortality. The final consideration for present purposes concerns the possible differentiation of valuations depending on variables such as age, gender, race, and location. Whilst the use of different valuations might yield results which more accurately reflect the influence of these variables on the economic standing of individuals, this is not done in this study, for the following reasons. Firstly, the empirical basis for introducing a wider range of valuations for different social groups, is weak. The only method would involve adjusting the above estimates for average incomes of each group being identified (in the same way as this was done in Table 5.1). However, this would introduce the same problems as are attributable to the human capital valuation approach:

particularly the ethical and equity considerations arising in policy decisions encompassing different social groups.

Secondly, the modelling of health outcomes does not permit differentiation between, for example, employed and unemployed victims of pollution. Thus it would not be possible to apply consistent valuation sets for the range of externalities being considered in this thesis. Finally, the marginal increase in 'accuracy' which might be achieved through further disaggregation of the above valuation sets, would require a disproportionately large increase in data collection and modelling sophistication. A subsequent section of this chapter will return to this issue in a critical assessment of the results and methodologies employed.

## Valuation of external costs in South Africa

In this section, valuations are derived for each of the five Class One externalities which were described in Chapter Four.

### Valuation of morbidity and mortality on coal mines

It was estimated in Chapter Four that the average fatality rate of coal-miners supplying the coal power stations was 0.156 per thousand GWh produced, equivalent to 23 deaths in 1994. The valuation of these deaths is shown in Table 5.2 below, in total Rands and in mills/kWh.[2]

| | Low estimate | Central estimate | High estimate |
|---|---|---|---|
| Total (Rm) | 16.1 | 23.0 | 32.2 |
| Total in mills/kWh | 0.11 | 0.16 | 0.22 |

**Table 5.2**  Valuation estimates for mortalities on coal mines, 1994

Although compensation amounts are paid to the families of killed miners, the amount being related to remuneration levels, these are not added to the valuation estimates for premature mortality, as the latter would already encompass any such cash payment.

With respect to injuries on the mines, the costs include the following main components: costs of medical treatment, opportunity costs of not working, and compensation costs paid to injured workers. Other costs, such as travel costs are not included in this calculation because, although relevant, they are small in relation to the other costs involved, and the fact that some of these costs have

---

2    One mill = 0.001 Rands (one-tenth of one cent).

to be estimated with no reference to empirical data does not warrant their inclusion.

Table 5.3 summarises the range of estimated opportunity costs for injuries. The medical costs will vary widely from case to case and no empirical data is available regarding these costs; consequently a range of estimates will be used, of R200, R1 000 and R2 000. For lost productivity, the number of days away from work (4, 8 and 12 weeks as discussed in Chapter Four) are valued at the average wage rate applicable on the coal mines. In 1993 this was R2 794 per month (CSS 1994: 4-16), which, if adjusted by 10% to 1994 levels, equates to R3 073 per month. Finally, compensation payments are based on the schedule of benefits stipulated in the Compensation for Occupational Injuries and Diseases Act, 1993 (Schedule 4). These payments are payable for temporary disablement, at a rate of 75% of the worker's monthly remuneration (up to a maximum of R6 669 per month). This compensation amounts to R2 305 per month and is payable for the period of absence from work. The injury statistics described in Chapter Four suggested that there would have been 131 injuries on the coal mines supplying Eskom in 1994. The results of applying the above cost estimates to this number of injuries are given in Table 5.3.

|  | *Low estimate* | *Central estimate* | *High estimate* |
|---|---|---|---|
| Medical costs | R26 200 | R131 000 | R262 000 |
| Lost productivity | R402 536 | R805 126 | R1 207 689 |
| Compensation payments | R301 955 | R603 910 | R905 734 |
| *Total cost* | R730 691 | R1 540 036 | R2 375 423 |
| *Cost in mills/kWh* | 0.005 | 0.010 | 0.016 |

**Table 5.3**   Valuation estimates for injuries on coal mines, 1994

The valuation of these impacts does not yield amounts of great significance when expressed as a cost per unit of electricity generated, even though the impacts can be highly significant at the local scale where they occur.

It should be noted that an important category of occupational morbidity has not been included in the above valuation estimates, namely the occurrence of respiratory and other diseases resulting from prolonged exposure of coal miners to high levels of dust and other airborne particulate matter. This externality was classified in Chapter Four as a Class Two impact, because, although its extent and economic value is considered to be significant, insufficient data exists at present to quantify it. Thus the effect of this omission will be to understate actual externality values.

## Valuation of water consumption in power stations

A review of the national pricing policy for bulk water supply was commenced in 1995, with a view to developing a policy which provides adequate signals to water consumers regarding the economic cost of water (DWAF 1995). By the end of 1995, no firm estimates had been made regarding marginal costing scenarios for water supply, although several values have been presented. One benchmark which is informing the policy debate is the cost of supplying water to the Highveld from the Lesotho Highlands Water Scheme. Again, some uncertainty exists regarding the economic cost of that water, especially because the feasibility studies are several years old; however, a value of R1.50 per m$^3$ has commonly been quoted. Some estimates of the economic cost of supplying additional water on the Highveld are higher, at about R3.00 per m$^3$, although there has been little analysis to underpin those estimate (Roome 1995). For purposes of this study, the central estimate of the economic value of water supplies by the power stations is R1.50 per m$^3$, with low and high values of R1.20 and R1.80 respectively. The external costs implicit in these water prices, expressed in terms of Rands per m$^3$ consumed, total Rands and mills/kWh of electricity generated, are shown in Table 5.4. The external costs are calculated with reference to the data in Table 4.3.

| | Low estimate | | Central estimate | | High estimate | |
|---|---|---|---|---|---|---|
| | R/m$^3$ | Rm | R/m$^3$ | Rm | R/m$^3$ | Rm |
| Arnot | 0.65 | 5.8 | 0.95 | 8.4 | 1.25 | 11.1 |
| Duvha | 0.61 | 25.0 | 0.91 | 37.3 | 1.21 | 49.6 |
| Hendrina | 0.80 | 21.8 | 1.10 | 29.9 | 1.40 | 38.1 |
| Kendal | 0.00 | 0.0 | 0.00 | 0.0 | 0.02 | 0.1 |
| Kriel | 0.41 | 13.5 | 0.71 | 23.4 | 1.01 | 33.2 |
| Lethabo | 1.08 | 32.7 | 1.38 | 43.6 | 1.68 | 53.1 |
| Matimba | 0.70 | 3.0 | 1.00 | 4.2 | 1.30 | 5.5 |
| Matla | 0.00 | 0.0 | 0.27 | 9.4 | 0.57 | 19.8 |
| Tutuka | 0.54 | 19.0 | 0.84 | 29.6 | 1.14 | 40.2 |
| Total value | | 120.8 | | 185.8 | | 250.7 |
| Average mills/kWh | | 0.82 | | 1.26 | | 1.69 |

**Table 5.4** Valuation estimates for water consumption external effects

The central estimate for the above calculation is that the externality – the under-pricing of water consumption – based on a marginal economic cost of R1.50 per m$^3$ of water, amounts to 0.13 cents per kWh on average. As noted in Chapter Four, water costs represent less than 2% of Eskom's operating costs (excluding depreciation and finance charges) so that even a large increase in the average price of water (127% in the case of the central estimate) would have a relatively small impact on electricity prices. This is discussed more fully later in this chapter.

## Valuation of health effects of power station air pollution emissions

The valuation of health effects resulting from air pollution emissions is the final step in the impact pathway analysis. As noted at the beginning of this chapter, the valuation approach adopted in this study is one based on the opportunity cost approach (as opposed to, for example, the willingness to pay method). Data exists regarding each of the main building blocks in the impact pathway – air pollution emissions, wind patterns, demographics, dose-response functions, and valuation data. To bring each of these together is a complex task and to this end a computer modelling tool, named EXMOD, has been utilised. EXMOD was developed over the period 1993-early 1995 for the New York State Environmental Externalities Cost Study, with support from the Empire State Electric Energy Research Corporation, the New York State Energy Research and Development Authority, the New York Department of Public Service and the Electric Power Research Institute. The aim of that study was to develop a user-friendly damage function tool with which impacts of new or relicensed electricity supply and demand management options could be evaluated. The work in the New York project was undertaken collaboratively by the Tellus Institute, Boston, and RCG/Hagler Bailly, Colorado and was summarised in four comprehensive volumes (Rowe et al 1993, 1994; Bernow et al 1995a, 1995b),[3] as well as a shorter paper (Rowe et al 1995). Following a review of international externalities studies, and particularly of models which could be of potential use in the South African context, EXMOD was investigated and selected for use in this study.

Briefly, the approach adopted in valuing health impacts was as follows. First, technical data about Eskom's nine coal power stations was collected and input into EXMOD; this data is summarised in Appendix 1, Tables A1 and A2. Data about fuel type and composition was also included. Second, demographic data was collected and arranged into a database file for each magisterial district in

---

3   All of these reports will be published in a two volume book by Oceana Press, New York State in 1996.

South Africa, from 1991 census data, including total population, age distribution, land area, geographical coordinates and average altitude of the district. Aggregated data was also obtained for the following neighbouring countries: Lesotho, Swaziland, Mozambique, Zimbabwe, Botswana and Namibia. Third, long-term surface wind data was obtained for fifteen monitoring stations in South Africa (and two in Namibia) and this was also entered into the appropriate database format. Fourth, emissions data was obtained from Eskom for each of its nine operational power stations for the main air pollutants: particulates, sulphur dioxide and nitrogen oxides (refer Table 4.5). Fifth, dose-response data from North America was used, as described in Tables 4.6 and 4.7, adjusted to reflect a higher degree of uncertainty in South Africa.

EXMOD was designed specifically to take all of this data into account and calculate the resultant damages, in physical terms (number of illnesses) and monetary terms (total damage costs or costs per kWh). The model is designed to estimate the damages associated with a *single* power facility (which can include coal, gas, nuclear, oil, DSM and other less common options). Consequently, the model was run nine times, corresponding to data sets for each of the nine operational coal power stations. It should be noted that EXMOD includes default data for every component of the impact pathway, as well as facility data and demographics; all of this was replaced with South African data, except for the dose-response functions and the atmospheric models -both of these issues were discussed earlier. Consequently, there is a reasonably good data set underlying this analysis.

The results of the model computations are summarised below. Table 5.5 shows the total physical health impacts, both in terms of morbidity and mortality, of air pollution emissions from all nine coal power stations. As noted earlier, this reflects actual emissions and demographics, and calculations regarding dispersion of pollutants and dose-response relationships. Several observations can be made regarding these physical health outcomes. Firstly, there is a reasonably wide range between the three estimates: this is appropriate given the uncertainty inherent in the modelling exercise. Secondly, the incidence of certain of these health outcomes is relatively high: notably, asthma attacks, respiratory symptom days and days of restricted activity. Asthma attacks are defined as a notable increase in asthma symptoms, such as shortness of breath, wheezing and use of more medication than normal. A relatively high proportion of the South African population – some 15% – suffers from asthma, which makes the results in Table 5.5 plausible. In the case of 'respiratory symptom days' the definition includes relatively minor symptoms of the respiratory system -coughs, colds, etc. Since these are not major illnesses, they have a correspondingly low monetary valuation (refer to Appendix 2). Likewise, 'restricted activity days' are defined as days which are spent in bed, away from work or on which normal activities cannot be performed.

| Health outcome | Unit | Low estimate | Cent. estimate | High estimate |
|---|---|---|---|---|
| Asthma attack | Occurrence-day | 525 900 | 1 405 300 | 1 920 100 |
| Acute bronchitis | Person | 3 535 | 6 927 | 11 292 |
| Chronic bronchitis | Person | 430 | 1 060 | 1 634 |
| Outpatient/GP visit | Visit | 2 477 | 6 044 | 8 862 |
| Mortality >65 | Death | 32 | 82 | 113 |
| Mortality <65 | Death | 24 | 92 | 153 |
| Resp. symptom day | Occurrence-day | 2 834 700 | 5 479 700 | 7 910 700 |
| Resp. hospital adm. | Admission | 360 | 672 | 962 |
| Restricted activity | Occurrence-day | 443 300 | 1 005 900 | 1 534 500 |

**Table 5.5** Physical health effects resulting from power station air
emissions, 1994 *(Source: EXMOD computations)*

Of more significance in Table 5.5, perhaps, are the number of mortalities
which are expected to occur in the base year: 82 in the population over 65
years, and 92 in those younger than 65 years (for the central estimate).
Normally, it is the older group which is more vulnerable to premature death
from pollution, and this is reflected in the dose-response relationships used in
the study. The reason for a higher estimate in the under-65 group, however, is
that South Africa's age distribution is bottom-heavy: less than 5% of the total
population is over 65 years of age, unlike industrialised countries, where the
latter group constitutes a much larger proportion of society. This analysis
suggests that 174 premature deaths will result from air pollution emissions from
power stations, with a low estimate of 56 and a high estimate of 266. This is
not insignificant, even in relation to the high population on the Highveld within
a few hundred kilometres of the power stations.

The results in Table 5.5 also highlight the burden of chronic and acute illness
which results from air pollution emissions: acute and chronic respiratory illnesses
which have relatively significant effects because of the medication and treatment
requirements, as well as lost productivity.

The physical health effects in Table 5.5 can be translated  into economic
values by calculating the average cost of each of these health outcomes. As
discussed at the beginning of this chapter, the methodology which has been
used is the cost of illness approach, which reflects direct opportunity costs of
the various health outcomes. The valuation data is described in more detail in
Appendix 2; the results of applying it to the physical health outcomes in the

previous table, are shown in Table 5.6. This table shows the range of estimates, in cents per kWh, of morbidity and mortality resulting from emissions of sulphur dioxide, nitrogen oxides and particulate matter.

| | Low estimate | | Central estimate | | High estimate | |
|---|---|---|---|---|---|---|
| | R/m | Mills/kWh | R/m | Mills/kWh | R/m | Mills/kWh |
| Arnot | 16.6 | 3.58 | 20.9 | 4.53 | 24.6 | 5.33 |
| Duvha | 82.4 | 3.74 | 117.0 | 5.3 | 146.0 | 6.62 |
| Hendrina | 66.8 | 5.66 | 85.5 | 7.24 | 101.0 | 8.57 |
| Kendal | 89.7 | 4.60 | 123.0 | 6.31 | 151.0 | 7.76 |
| Kriel | 69.4 | 5.15 | 101.0 | 7.53 | 128.0 | 9.52 |
| Lethabo | 84.9 | 4.78 | 116.0 | 6.51 | 142.0 | 7.97 |
| Matimba | 40.0 | 1.77 | 51.4 | 2.27 | 61.0 | 2.70 |
| Matla | 77.0 | 4.11 | 110.0 | 5.87 | 138.0 | 7.35 |
| Tutuka | 55.9 | 3.19 | 80.1 | 4.57 | 100.0 | 5.73 |
| Weighted av. / Total value | 582.7 | 3.94 | 804.9 | 5.43 | 991.6 | 6.70 |

**Table 5.6** Valuation of morbidity and mortality from power station emissions,1994
*(Source: EXMOD computations)*

The valuation results for the nine coal power stations are of a similar order of magnitude, with total damages of R805 million in the central estimate (R583 m and R992 m for the low and high estimates). These translate into external costs of 5.43 mills or 0.543 cents per kWh in the central case. The lowest damages in absolute terms arose from Arnot power station, which was operating only two of six sets during 1994. In relation to electricity output, the lowest external costs resulted from Matimba power station with a central estimate of 2.27 mills/kWh, due to the fact that it is located in a sparsely-densely populated area in Northern Province. The highest damages in total Rand amounts arose from Kendal, Duvha and Lethabo, the first two having high emission rates for sulphur dioxide, and the latter being close to relatively large towns along the Vaal River. As a unit of electricity output, Kriel and Hendrina have the highest external costs, probably because their nitrogen oxide and particulate emission factors, respectively, were relatively high (based on 1994 emissions).

It should be noted, once again, that these valuations exclude Class Two damages which have not been quantified, such as damages resulting from acidic deposition or impaired visibility. Thus there is certainty over the direction of at least one source of bias in these estimates, namely that the estimates will under-state some external effects.

### Valuation of damages from greenhouse gas emissions

As noted in Chapter Four, there is considerable scientific uncertainty about the damages which are likely to result globally from anthropogenic emissions of greenhouse gases. The economic estimation of the scale of these damages -resulting from, for example, changing rainfall patterns, sea level rise and more frequent weather extremes – is a relatively young area of study. A number of studies have attempted to make estimates of the orders of magnitude of these damages: a wide range of estimates has been made, and not surprisingly, there is disagreement over a number of assumptions in these estimates.

One of the most recent estimates has been made by Working Group 3 of the Intergovernmental Panel on Climate Change, the body of leading social and natural scientists informing the international negotiation process. Their analysis has suggested that the annual costs of global warming will be in the region of 1.5% to 2% of gross world product (GWP) by the time $CO_2$ concentrations reach double their natural levels – somewhere around 2050 or 2060 on the basis of current trends. Notably, this analysis has been criticised by some economists as being too conservative, with alternative estimates of global costs being in the range of 12% to 130% of GWP by 2050 (Meyer & Cooper 1995).

By relating global damage costs to current emissions of GHGs, it is possible to estimate a cost per ton of GHG, or more particularly, $CO_2$ emissions. Corresponding with the high level of uncertainty over future damage costs, there is an equally wide range of 'per ton' damage cost scenarios. The IPCC, in its 1995 Second Assessment Report, 'does not endorse any particular range of values for the marginal damage of $CO_2$ emissions', but instead referred to published estimates which fall into the range of $5 to $125 per ton (IPCC 1995). One such estimate, by Fankhauser and Pearce (1993), both of whom were centrally involved in this aspect of the IPCC Working Group III's work, amounted to 14 Pounds per ton of $CO_2$, equivalent to R80 or $22 per ton (reported in Pearce 1995: 31). This value will be used as the central estimate in this study. For the low estimate, the lowest value referred to in the IPCC report will be used: $5 per ton, equivalent to R18 per ton. The choice of a high value is made more complicated by the wide range of estimates which have been published. The high value referred to by the IPCC, of $125 per ton, will not be used here since it is far in excess of most valuations which have been published to date (see for example Rowe et al 1994b; Nordhaus 1991) which are mostly in the range of $5 to $20 per ton. For present purposes, the high estimate of damages will be taken (arbitrarily) as being 50% higher than the central estimate, that is, R120 per ton (or nearly $33 per ton).

To summarise, therefore, the three values used in this study are R18, R80 and R120 per ton of $CO_2$. On this basis, the estimates of damages which may result from South African power station emissions of GHGs (as summarised in Table 3.12) are shown in Table 5.7.

| | Low estimate (Rm) | Central est. (Rm) | High estimate (Rm) |
|---|---|---|---|
| Total value (Rm) | 2 572.2 | 11 432.0 | 17.148 |
| Average mills/kWh | 17.38 | 77.24 | 115.86 |

**Table 5-7** Valuation estimates for $CO_2$ -induced climate change damages

It is evident from the calculations in the table that at any of the unit damage costs, global damage costs attributable to GHG emissions from the South African power sector are highly material. For the central estimate, external costs are in the region of 7.7 c/kWh, which is very significant in relation to current electricity prices. The policy implications of this are *not* simply that these costs should be internalised into the price of coal-fired electricity, since there would be no benefit for South Africa of doing so if other emitters of GHGs did not (the 'free rider' problem). Rather, the policy response will depend on the international regimes being negotiated in terms of the Framework Convention on Climate Change, which explicitly recognises the differential responsibilities of industrialised and developing countries in the mitigation of climate change impacts. This issue will be addressed further in Chapter Six.

# Valuation of subsidies to nuclear industry

The production of nuclear electricity in South Africa involves two kinds of externalities: environmental and fiscal effects. In Chapter Four it was established that, while environmental externalities may be significant, there is insufficient information to value them in this study. Fiscal externalities, however, were classified as a Class One impact. The cumulative subsidy which was directed to the nuclear industry from 1971 to 1995 amounted to R21 753.3 million (in 1995 Rands – refer to Table 4.9), of which R12 298 million was estimated to be related to the production of electricity. In order to calculate an average external cost, this subsidy should be spread, as far as possible, over the lifetime of the assets to which they are related.

There is currently some uncertainty over the future of Koeberg power station and the Atomic Energy Corporation. Thus three scenarios will be used for purpose of calculating the fiscal externality:

- *Low estimate:* the subsidy ceases from 1996/97 onwards and the power station operates at full capacity until 2023.
- *Central estimate:* the subsidy is phased out from its current level to zero by the year 2000,[4] while operations remain at their current level.
- *High estimate:* support for the industry terminates and production of electricity ceases at the end of 1996.

Table 5.8 summarises the external costs for each of these three scenarios; subsidy figures are drawn from Chapter Four and Auf der Heyde (1993, 1995), whilst electricity generation figures are based on actual production since the power station was commissioned, and assumed output for the remainder of its forty year life at 1995 levels. Under any of these three scenarios, it is clear that the nuclear sector has benefited from a highly significant fiscal subsidy which has not been reflected in the price of nuclear electricity. Clearly, a portion of the fiscal allocation to the nuclear industry has not been used to *produce* electricity – for example, the costs of operating the Council for Nuclear Safety – but this is not the point. What is relevant is that none of these costs would have been incurred if South Africa had not developed its nuclear capacity, and even the costs of maintaining safety standards are external costs related to the production of nuclear electricity. Consequently, their evaluation as an externality is consistent with economic theory.

|  | Low estimate | Central estimate | High estimate |
|---|---|---|---|
| Total subsidy (Rm 1995) | R12 298 | R12 995 | R12 298 |
| Cumulative generation (GWh) | 370 848 | 370 848 | 109 029 |
| External cost, mills/kWh | 33.16 | 35.04 | 112.80 |

**Table 5.8** Valuation of fiscal externalities in the nuclear industry

It should also be noted that the central scenario assumes that subsidy allocations to the nuclear industry will be scaled down to zero by 2000 – consistent with the so-called 'AEC 2000 plus' business plan. The trend in the 1995/96 and 1996/97 budget allocations does not appear to be in line with this vision, however – rather, the subsidy has not been reduced to the extent envisaged in the AEC's own business plan, which means the central estimate may understate the amount of the fiscal externality.

---

4    Thus the allocation to the electricity component of the industry is assumed to be 57% of the annual allocations: R489.2 million for 1996/97, R366.9 million for 1997/98, R244.6 million for 1998/99, and R122.3 million in 1999/2000 (all in 1995 Rands).

# Summary of valuation results

The combined effect of valuing the five Class One externalities is summarised in Table 5.9. The estimates reflect the results of the valuation exercise undertaken in this study; as noted earlier, only the most important externalities, for which there is sufficient information, have been quantified in this study. Consequently, the valuations constitute an incomplete estimate of the external costs of electricity generation in South Africa and, as such, reflect a *minimum* estimate. Table 5.9 also summarises the level of uncertainty related to each of the externality valuations, taking into account the reliability of the data sources and the completeness of information about various stages in the impact pathway. It should be noted that the valuations in Table 5.9 are not additive, since they do not have a common base: they are expressed in relation to the amount of coal and nuclear electricity generated, respectively.

|  | Level of uncertainty | Low estimate | Central estimate | High estimate |
|---|---|---|---|---|
| Coal mining: injuries & mortalities[1] | *moderate* | *0.12* | *0.17* | *0.24* |
| Generation: water consumption | *moderate* | *0.82* | *1.26* | *1.69* |
| Generation: air pollution & health impacts[2] | *moderate* | *3.94* | *5.43* | *6.70* |
| Generation: greenhouse gases | *high* | *17.38* | *77.24* | *115.86* |
| Nuclear: fiscal subsidy moderate | *moderate* | *33.16* | *35.04* | *112.80* |
| Coal mining: air & water pollution | *high* | *nq*[3] | *nq* | *nq* |
| Generation: air pollution & acidification | *high* | *nq* | *nq* | *nq* |
| Generation: air pollution & visibility | *high* | *nq* | *nq* | *nq* |
| Generation: water quality impacts | *high* | *nq* | *nq* | *nq* |
| Nuclear: environmental and health | *high* | *nq* | *nq* | *nq* |

**Notes**
1. The external costs of coal miners' morbidity (chronic and acute illness) have not been quantified because insufficient information exists regarding their pollution exposures.
2. The external costs of health impacts caused by pollution originating from ash dumps on the power stations have not been quantified because insufficient information exists regarding the quantity of emissions and their dispersal.
3. 'nq': not quantified, either because uncertainty is too high or because impacts are not considered to be highly material.

**Table 5.9** Summary of valuation results for Class One and Class Two externalities in 1994, mills/kWh

Summarising the Class One externalities in Table 5.9, totals can be derived for the coal and nuclear cycles, and for an average of both. These results are shown in Table 5.10. The weighted average external cost takes into account the relative proportions of coal and nuclear electricity generated by Eskom.

|  | Low est. | Central est. | High est. |
|---|---|---|---|
| Total coal fuel cycle | 22.26 | 84.10 | 124.49 |
| Nuclear: fiscal subsidy | 33.16 | 35.04 | 112.80 |
| Weighted average external cost | 22.93 | 81.08 | 123.78 |

**Table 5.10**  Summary of externality valuations for coal and nuclear cycles in mills/kWh, 1994

The central estimate for all Class One externalities included in this study is therefore 81.08 mills/kWh (8.1 c/kWh, with a lower bound of 22.93 mills/kWh and an upper estimate of 123.78 mills/kWh. It is evident that the highest external costs are attributable to greenhouse gas emissions and the fiscal subsidy for the nuclear industry. If both of these are ignored, then the central estimate of damages is 6.86 mills/kWh (0.69 c/kWh), with low and high ranges of 4.88 mills/kWh and 8.63 mills/kWh respectively.

These results can be placed into context by comparing them with current electricity price levels. The relative significance of the externalities obviously varies depending on the choice of a benchmark tariff. For present purposes, three of Eskom's tariffs can be used: its average industrial tariff, the prepayment domestic (S1) tariff and the weighted average tariff for all consumers. These tariffs at the end of 1994, were 10.06 mills/kWh, 25.81 mills/kWh and 11.76 mills/kWh respectively (all inclusive of 14% VAT, Eskom 1995a: 2, 1994: 26). The results of this comparison are shown in Table 5.11.

|  | Low est. | Central est. | High est. |
|---|---|---|---|
| Average industrial tariff | 23% | 81% | 123% |
| Low-income domestic (S1) tariff | 9% | 31% | 48% |
| Average Eskom tariff | 19% | 69% | 105% |

**Table 5.11**  Average external cost as a percentage of industrial, prepayment domestic and average tariffs, 1994

Table 5.12 makes the same comparison, but this time compared only to Eskom's average tariff for 1994, and with a breakdown for each of the five Class One externalities. This makes it possible to evaluate the effect on prices of any combination of these externalities. For instance, if the damage costs related to greenhouse gas emissions were ignored for reasons of uncertainty or in response to developments in the international political arena, then the central estimate for the externalities would amount to 7% of average prices for 1994. Likewise, if nuclear externalities are ignored, then the central estimate of external effects would be 67% of average price levels.[5]

|  | Low est. | Central est. | High est. |
|---|---|---|---|
| Coal mining: injuries & mortalities | 0.1% | 0.1% | 0.2% |
| Generation: water consumption | 0.7% | 1.0% | 1.3% |
| Generation: air pollution & health impacts | 3.1% | 4.3% | 5.3% |
| Generation: greenhouse gases | 13.9% | 61.6% | 92.5% |
| Nuclear: fiscal subsidy | 1.7% | 1.8% | 5.9% |
| Total | 19.5% | 68.9% | 105.3% |

**Table 5.12** Average Class One externalities as a percentage of Eskom's average tariffs, 1994

The results in Table 5.12 show the relative importance of the Class One externalities taking into account the relative mix of coal and nuclear electricity, in relation to average tariffs for 1994. Because nuclear electricity accounted for just over 6% of the coal-nuclear total, its relative impact on electricity prices becomes much smaller than when compared to nuclear-generated electricity alone. Much more significant in this comparison is the impact of assumed damage costs from climate change representing 62% of average tariffs in the central case. Of the environmental externalities experienced within the country and its neighbours in the relatively short term, health impacts of air emissions are most significant, representing between 3% and 5% of current electricity prices.

It is worth making a brief comparison of the results of this analysis with the results of externality studies undertaken elsewhere – as summarised in Chapter Three, Table 3.1. The valuations in this study fall somewhere between the two main sets of externality values derived internationally: perhaps closer to the lower, more recent bottom-up studies in the second half of Table 3.1. This seems consistent with expectations: on the one hand, it would be expected that the

---

5    From the perspective of economic theory, it would be interesting to construct the marginal external cost (MEC) and marginal social cost (MSC) curves implied by these calculations – as outlined in Chapter Two.

external costs in South Africa might be higher than those in Europe or North America where emissions standards and environmental controls are generally much stricter. On the other hand, this study excluded many externalities for which there was insufficient data, which would be expected to result in lower valuation results here. In conclusion, the results of the present study, albeit subject to a number of limitations which are outlined below, appear plausible on the basis of international experience.

## Limitations and weaknesses in study

It is important in quantitative analysis such as this to stress that the calculated figures are as good only as the input assumptions and information from which they are derived. By its nature, any externalities study is subject to a number of limitations and weaknesses, which mean that the economic values which are calculated should not be taken simply at face value. Rather, they should be analysed in full awareness of the limitations of the study, of which there are three main categories: omissions, uncertainties and biases.

Firstly, in the case of omissions, several Class Two and Class Three impacts were not quantified in the present study. Class Two impacts were those which were considered to be potentially serious, but for which there was insufficient information to permit an economic valuation to be made. It would be important, therefore, in a more complete analysis, to include these impacts as well:

- chronic and acute illnesses experienced by workers on coal mines supplying Eskom;
- impacts of air and water pollution emitted by coal mines supplying the power stations;
- impacts on human health of air pollution originating from coal power stations' ash dumps;
- impacts of coal power station emissions and resultant acidic deposition, in terms of human health, damages to crops, forests, water supplies and other physical assets in the Mpumalanga Highveld and neighbouring regions;
- impacts of coal power station emissions on visibility conditions, particularly in the Mpumalanga Highveld;
- impacts of coal power station emissions into water courses on the quality of resources;
- impacts of nuclear power stations on environmental quality and human health.

It is possible that the economic value of some of these externalities will be significant and they therefore warrant further investigation. In addition to these issues, it is possible that some of the externalities which were accorded a Class Three rating in this study could have significant economic values. For instance, it is possible that aesthetic impacts of power stations, substations and high-voltage transmission lines, could be significant for some social groups or in some areas; likewise society's valuation of the health impacts of electro-magnetic fields (EMFs) could be significant in aggregate, even though there is conflicting scientific evidence regarding their effect on human health. Ideally, all of these Class Three effects should be subjected to a more comprehensive analysis.

In respect of uncertainties in the present analysis, Table 5.9 summarised the level of uncertainty for each of the Class One and Two impacts, at a very broad level. It is worth describing briefly the most significant areas of uncertainty in respect of the five main externalities which were quantified in this study:

- Firstly, in the case of injuries and deaths occurring in the coal-mining sector, data for the coal mining industry as a whole had to be apportioned between the main consumers, since data was not available specifically for the coal mines supplying Eskom. The effect of this may have been either to understate or overstate the results.

- Secondly, there is uncertainty over the applicability of dose-response functions derived in North America to South African populations. No epidemiological studies have yet derived these relationships for South Africa.

- With regard to the valuation of health impacts of air pollution, there is a moderate level of uncertainty regarding the atmospheric modelling approach used. The EXMOD model used a Gaussian plume type of dispersion model to approximate the dispersion of emissions from power station chimneys, whereas actual conditions on the Highveld are not especially well-represented by this kind of model (Turner 1995). In the absence of any atmospheric model designed specifically for South African conditions, however, this level of uncertainty is unavoidable.

- Fourthly, there is a high level of uncertainty regarding the future global impacts of anthropogenic greenhouse gas emissions in the economic, social and environmental spheres.

- Finally, there has been very little previous analysis of the economic value of environmental.and health issues, from the pricing of water to the value of human health and mortality, and consequently there is a high level of uncertainty in this respect.

These uncertainties have been accommodated, to an extent, by utilising a range of estimates rather than a single estimate, and by allocating an appropriate weighting to these estimates where relevant, so as to reflect the inherent uncertainty. In most of the cases above, there would be benefits to undertaking further investigation to narrow the range of uncertainty.

It is important to be explicit about the effect of these omissions and uncertainties on the economic valuations which have been reported in this study, that is, whether the direction of the resultant *bias* will be to understate or overstate the externality valuations. A summary of these potential biases is shown in Table 5.13.

| Uncertainty or omission | Direction of bias on externality values | | |
|---|---|---|---|
| | Understated | Unknown | Overstated |
| Class Two & Three impacts omitted (refer above list) | x | | |
| Coal mine accident rates: industry average vs. Eskom suppliers rates | | ? | |
| Dose-response functions: North American vs. South African data | x | ? | |
| Atmospheric dispersion modelling | | ? | |
| Future impacts of GHG emissions | | ? | |
| Valuation of environmental and health impacts | | ? | |

**Table 5.13**  Summary of potential biases in this study due to omissions and uncertainties

The overall effect of these biases is difficult to assess, since any one of them (for example, GHG impacts) could be large enough to more than offset all others. Nonetheless, it is important to note that there is one definite source of bias: namely the omission of Class One and Two impacts, which would cause estimates to understate actual impacts. In all cases in this study, the chosen route has been to err on the side of understating external effects rather than the opposite. Thus there is a fairly high level of confidence that the range of quantified externalities does not overstate the *minimum* value of externalities in the South African power sector.

# 6

# Policy implications

Cheap electricity is an important comparative advantage for South Africa, both as a foundation for economic growth and as a basis for extending poor households' access to affordable electricity services. The results of this study, however, suggest that the full costs of producing coal and nuclear electricity are somewhat higher than the costs borne directly by the electricity industry. These external costs are not fictitious: they are paid by society as a whole – be it through health expenditure, taxes directed to the industry or *de facto* subsidisation of resources. To this extent, therefore, electricity prices are artificially low. This is not to deny that there are also sound economic reasons which explain the low price: the abundance of coal reserves (close to power stations), the high level of technological expertise in the generation sector, and the financial strength of the national utility. The point, rather, is that there are fairly significant hidden costs which are not reflected in the price of electricity.

The policy implications of this are complex. From a purely theoretical perspective, the appropriate response would be to 'internalise' these costs, possibly through instruments such as pollution taxes, tradable emission permits, or through more stringent environmental regulation. The aim, in theory, would be either to reduce external costs (by, for instance, removing the subsidies) or to reflect them in the price of electricity. In practice, however, this is a difficult task. Importantly, the analysis in this study should *not* be interpreted to suggest (simplistically) that South Africa's electricity should be made more expensive than it currently is. Indeed, there is no single policy response which will adequately deal with the diverse range of externalities quantified in this report. Rather, more specific responses are required in respect of each area; this chapter outlines a number of key policy implications.

## A first estimate of baseline external costs

In effect, the analysis in this report represents a first (and by no means conclusive) attempt to value the external costs of electricity generation in South Africa. This is useful for several purposes. Firstly, it represents a baseline against which comparisons can be made in the future. If, for instance, environmental policies are introduced with a view to reducing air pollution concentrations, progress can be evaluated in the future in economic terms, by comparing with the 1994 baseline produced in this report.

Secondly, the valuation of external costs is a necessary component of any cost-benefit analyses of abatement options which may be considered. Thus, for instance, an assessment of the relative costs and benefits of utilising technologies with lower sulphur emissions (such as scrubbers or fluidised bed combustion), will include the costs of those technologies as well as the benefits. These benefits will, simplistically, be equal to the avoided external costs. To the extent that this study includes some of these externalities, it provides one of the basic building blocks for such a cost-benefit analysis. In more theoretical terms, an external cost curve could be derived from the valuations in this report, and this could be plotted against the abatement cost curves, to find the socially optimal level of production or pollution.

Thirdly, quantification of external costs is an essential component of integrated resource planning (IRP). IRP is a planning approach in which all energy supply and demand options are evaluated with a view to making the resource choice which is optimal from the view of society as a whole.[1] Typically, IRP assessments compare energy supply investments (such as building another coal power station, or importing hydro-electricity) with demand-side management options and seek to make the comparison on an equal footing. Since the private costs and external costs of these options vary widely, it is important to include *all* costs in such comparisons. Therefore, when Eskom makes its next decision about how to satisfy the country's electricity needs, it should do this on the basis of *full* cost comparisons: in other words, the social (private plus external) cost of another coal power station should be compared with the social cost of a gas power station, imported hydro-electricity, demand-side management, and so on. The present study has provided a first-order indication of the main external costs of coal and nuclear electricity.

## The pursuit of low electricity prices

Eskom's vision is to 'provide the world's lowest-cost electricity for growth and prosperity' (Eskom 1995: i). This vision, by itself, might not best serve the country's interests. It would be quite possible for South Africa to be the world's cheapest electricity producer if, for instance, it paid no regard whatsoever to

---

1    IRP is widely used in North America, where electricity regulators stipulate that utilities have to undertake an IRP assessment of all the options they face for meeting demand. These assessments typically include quantification of external costs.

environmental conditions and polluted the environment freely.[2] In essence, such a situation would amount to a subsidy being granted to the industry by the environment – in both its natural and social dimensions. This kind of subsidy is as unsustainable as the large fiscal subsidies which many utilities in Latin America and Africa received from their governments, notably during the 1970s and 1980s.

It is obvious that Eskom does not act in single-minded pursuit of low-cost electricity without regard for the environmental consequences of its actions. It has invested in technologies to reduce its impact on its surroundings (for example, electrostatic precipitators), and it incurs ongoing expenditure on the management of its impacts. It reported in its first 'Environmental Report' that approximately R135 million was spent on environmental management and research during 1994 (1995b: 35). Over half of this was on air quality management in the generation division (Roos 1995). The relevant question, rather, relates to the *degree* to which environmental considerations are taken on board in the pursuit of cheap electricity. Clearly, there are external costs associated with producing electricity and 'artificially' low prices provide a powerful but dangerous signal to electricity consumers. It is not difficult to imagine a scenario in which major electricity-intensive industries establish themselves in South Africa in response to low electricity prices (all other things equal), but that some years later the environmental costs become too large to ignore. At that point, the clean-up costs and control costs could be significant and would probably translate into an unavoidable price shock. Thus the original vision – being the lowest-cost producer in the world – would be severely compromised, with potentially adverse economic effects.

This scenario is offered in order to highlight the potential problems which may arise if the stated vision is interpreted too literally or narrowly. It is important, therefore, that Eskom's vision be tempered by its stewardship responsibilities to the natural and social environments. Part of this responsibility is to account for the full costs of its activities.

## Policies to respond to the electricity industry's external costs

This study identified five externalities which were significant and for which valuation estimates were made. Although the main focus of this study is not on the policy implications of each of these areas, it is important to at least provide an indication of the policy responses which are already occurring or which are required.

---

2   The philosophy of China and certain newly-industrialised countries in South-east Asia is sometimes characterised in this way.

## Injuries and mortality in the coal mines

The safety performance of South African mines in general, including coal mines, was heavily criticised by the Leon Commission. It was the Commission's view that the number of injuries and fatalities was 'unacceptably high' (1995: 16). Many aspects of this issue were addressed by the Commission, and views were presented to it by labour, management, researchers, and other stakeholders in the sector. It is not the intention here to repeat the range of recommendations made by the Leon Commission, nor to describe actions taken subsequent to its release. The relevant point for present purposes is to note that many of these costs (in terms of injury, illness and premature death) have not been accounted for in the price of coal – nor, therefore, in the price of electricity. More attention to worker health and safety in the coal mines, whether this is driven by stricter regulations, union demands or management initiatives, should have the effect of reducing accidents. To the extent that this results in incremental costs being incurred by the industry, it is most likely that a very large proportion of these will be passed on to consumers, meaning, ultimately, upward pressure on electricity prices. In economic terms, this is entirely correct: consumers should be aware of, and should pay for, the full implications of their consumption behaviour.

## The pricing of water consumed in power stations

The country's bulk water pricing policy is currently under review, and it is not the intention here to pre-empt the results of that process. Nonetheless, it is certain that the historical cost of supplying water to the power stations bears no relation to the current economic value of that water. As such, Eskom is not being given the correct price signals regarding its consumption patterns and, as a result, its technology choices do not necessarily take account of water scarcity. Only two of its coal power stations, Kendal and Matimba, employ dry cooling technologies. The appropriate policy would be for bulk water supply authorities – generally the Department of Water Affairs and Forestry – to move away from historic cost pricing, towards economic pricing of water. As noted in Chapter Five, the increase of estimated economic water prices and current prices amounts to 127%, which is a large increase to absorb without causing electricity price shocks, notwithstanding the fact that water accounts for less than 2% of operating costs at present.

If water prices more than double, this will have a noticeable effect on electricity prices, and so it is important that new pricing policies are introduced in a well-planned and phased manner. At the very least, marginal cost pricing structures should be implicit in the planning and feasibility studies for any new power stations which are under consideration. For existing facilities, a phased introduction of economic prices should be agreed upon in advance, so that unexpected price effects can be minimised as far as possible. It is important to note, however, that the main objective, ultimately, is for prices to be set at a sufficiently high level to reflect the scarcity of water, so there is a limit to the concessions which can or should be made for water consumers. As a consumer which is guaranteed the most secure water supplies, even in times of drought, it is correct that Eskom (and its customers) should pay for that privilege.

### Health effects of air pollution emissions

The analysis of the external costs of air pollution emissions on human health suggested that they are in the region of 0.54 cents per kWh (range: 0.39 to 0.67 c/kWh). The central estimate represents approximately 4% of average electricity tariffs in the same base year. Significantly, this estimate excludes a large number of externalities which may have significant costs, notably the long-term effects of acidification on buildings, crops, forests and other objects at ground level. There are numerous policy approaches which can be employed to address these external effects, including the setting of emissions limits, the specification of control technologies to be used, the introduction of pollution taxes or tradable emissions permits, and self-regulation by polluters. It is beyond the scope of the present study to analyse all of these options and to propose suitable policies. Nonetheless, it is possible to make explicit some key implications of the analysis made here.

First, the order of magnitude of the health costs which currently occur are not insignificant and may merit consideration of abatement measures. Taking as a point of departure the current stock of coal power stations, the range of technical options for reducing gaseous and particulate emissions is relatively narrow. Commonly discussed in this regard are flue-gas scrubbers, which could be retrofitted to existing power stations. There has not been any thorough public investigation to date of the economics of this technology option. Eskom's position on this has been that the costs of retrofitting its power stations with scrubbers are prohibitively high, at anything from 33% to 49% of prices (King & Rodseth 1993: 20), and that with costs of this order of magnitude, it is more effective to invest in electrification in highly-polluted townships (Lennon & Turner 1992: 5). Clearly, there are constraints on capital and investment resources which mean that investment decisions need to weigh up all alternatives, but it may be misleading to present air pollution abatement options as a direct trade-off between power station controls and electrification. Experience in recent years has shown that urban electrification does not lead to significant pollution reduction, and much less rural electrification. The national electrification programme is certainly not motivated by environmental concerns.

In assessing whether pollution abatement technologies are justifiable in economic terms, two sides of the equation need to be considered. The first is the *cost of abatement*; Eskom's analysis suggests that this would lead to increases in electricity prices in the region of 30-50%. This estimate is somewhat higher than experience elsewhere suggests – see for example, Petrie et al (1992: 434) in which international experience regarding this cost penalty was reported to be in the region of 10-15% – but it is clear that the cost penalty will be in the region of 10-30%.[3] The second part of the equation is the *benefit of abatement*, and this will consist primarily of the avoided environmental costs. The analysis in this study suggests that current health costs represent in the region of 4% of electricity prices. It could be expected that these costs would be reduced by 70-90% depending on the abatement technologies adopted; in addition, abatement benefits would also be felt in other areas not quantified in this study, such as reduced costs of acidification. It appears, therefore, from the orders of magnitude mentioned here, that the costs of abatement options do not necessarily outweigh the benefits by a large margin, especially if non-quantified externalities are included in this calculation.

A range of technological options exist to reduce air pollution emissions; flue gas scrubbers are the best-known of these, but not necessarily the best option from an economic or environmental perspective. A more promising option is fluidised bed combustion; although this is a relatively young technology, life cycle cost analyses suggest that its performance is better than flue gas desulphurisation in most respects (Diekmann & Notten 1995). Possibly of great significance in South Africa's dry conditions, is that scrubbers require large quantities of water for ongoing operations, and in the context of increasing water scarcity and higher water prices, this represents a serious barrier.

With regard to fiscal instruments such as pollution taxes or tradable emissions permits, it would make little sense from an economic or environmental perspective to impose such instruments only on Eskom's power stations, without including other major sources of pollution. For such instruments to be adopted, an integrated policy is required in which *all* major pollution sources are included. Thus, in the absence of such a framework, this is not a feasible policy option at present.

To conclude this discussion, the point here is not to propose technical solutions to air pollution problems, nor even to suggest that abatement options are economically justifiable. It is, rather, is that the current scale of environmental and health costs is of an order of magnitude which warrants serious consideration of new abatement options. Any such analysis should take a wider view than has been the case to date, and needs to take full account of all current environmental and health costs which may be reduced by available abatement options.

---

3    Clearly, variations in the base cost of electricity (the denominator) will influence the amount of the percentage increase.

## Emission of greenhouse gases

The international governance of greenhouse gas emissions, and mitigation of their effects, is a rapidly evolving arena. The current situation is that South Africa, if and when it ratifies the Framework Convention on Climate Change (FCCC), will not face any specific emission reduction targets or obligations. For the present, and at least for the next few years, these commitments are likely to fall only on industrialised countries. Even in their cases, it is left up to the individual countries (or the European Union, which has also ratified the Convention) to decide on the most cost-effective ways of achieving their targets. A handful, for example, have introduced taxes on carbon emissions or energy consumption, or a combination of both. In other countries, these options have been ruled out for the time being. There is no immediate necessity for South Africa to introduce GHG mitigation measures at its own expense. A range of international funding sources exist to assist developing countries achieve reductions in their GHG emissions – for example, the Global Environment Facility (GEF) administered by the World Bank, and unilateral funding from (inter alia) Germany and the United States. These sources are available, at present, to assist developing countries to fulfil their reporting requirements in terms of the FCCC, as well as to support projects that have benefits for the global environment.

It is clear from the international scenario around climate change policies that there is no question, for the present, of introducing a carbon tax or similar externality 'adder' on South Africa's carbon dioxide emissions. This does not mean, however, that South Africa can afford to ignore the climate change issue. As noted in Chapter Four, this country was the eighteenth-largest source of GHG emissions in 1988, and one of the largest on a per capita basis. The energy sector is the single largest source within South Africa; it therefore has some responsibility to consider the effect of emissions. Also, it is possible that middle-income developing countries such as South Africa will face stricter commitments at some point in the not-too-distant future. If this is the case, then it would be imprudent to ignore the relative impacts of different electricity supply options in terms of their climate change implications.

The quantification of externalities in Chapter Five made it abundantly clear that the potential scale of damages is very large, and so the relative cost of more $CO_2$-intensive energy sources will be considerably higher than other alternatives. This factor could be highly consequential when decisions are taken around the country's next bulk supply option, given that coal is much more carbon-intensive than hydro-electricity or gas. In industrialised countries, this factor is playing a significant role in investment and planning decisions about resource development in the energy sector.

## Subsidies to the nuclear industry

The analysis of the fiscal externality which flows from public funds to the nuclear industry showed that this amount ranged from 3.3 to 11.3 c/kWh, depending on the assumptions made about the future of the industry. Even in the most optimistic scenario, the subsidy represents more than half the current average price of electricity. On this basis, it is clear that nuclear electricity has historically been heavily subsidised, and will continue to be until the end of the life of Koeberg power station.

The externality calculations in this study reflect the *average* external costs. From an economic point of view, an analysis of future policy options should be concerned with *marginal* costs of various alternatives. Thus the subsidy to the industry over the past 25 years is a 'sunk cost': it has been expended and cannot be recovered. Policy analyses regarding the nuclear industry should concern themselves with the cost-effectiveness of future investments and expenditure from public resources, and with the marginal environmental impact of future operations. Thus the central question for policy-making purposes is whether the advantages of continuing to operate the country's nuclear facilities outweigh their disadvantages. Importantly, this analysis should be comprehensive and take into account all the future economic, environmental, social and other impacts related to the various options. In economic terms, all of the private and external costs should be included in the calculation; the latter include, for instance, society's valuation of risks of environmental hazards, catastrophes and so on. The absolute scale of subsidies which have historically been granted to the industry appear, from the results in Chapter Five, to be so large as to make it highly unlikely that they can be justified on economic grounds, especially when there are so many other sources of electricity in the region. Of course, factors other than economically quantifiable ones will also enter the decision.

A comprehensive investigation of the nuclear industry and its various components was, in fact, called for at the ANC's Conference on Nuclear Policy in February 1994 (EMG & ANC 1994), and is listed as one of the options in the government's Energy Policy Discussion Document (DMEA 1995: 150).

# Energy efficiency and demand-side management policy responses

This study has focused almost exclusively on the supply side – in other words, on the generation of electricity. Whilst this focus has been deliberate, it is important to flag the demand side of the industry and, in particular, the possible benefits from implementing energy efficiency and demand-side management (DSM) policies. Clearly, policy responses aimed at internalising or managing externalities will bring about upward pressure on electricity prices. If, however, energy efficiency interventions are adopted at the same time, the potential exists to offset any such price increases, and, indeed, sustain current downward trends. Internationally, electricity utilities have invested in energy efficiency and DSM programmes over the past decade or more, partly in response to public and regulatory pressures to reduce the environmental costs of generating electricity from coal and other fossil fuels. In South Africa, there has been relatively little attention paid to the demand side of the equation, partly as a result of the over-capacity situation in Eskom's coal power stations. Eskom has recently established a demand-side management programme, although it remains a relatively low investment priority for the organisation. Nonetheless, indications are that considerable energy savings can be achieved, at low or negative cost, through the adoption of well-proven technologies and practices. For example, considerable savings can be made in the household sector by improving the thermal performance of low-cost houses which are being connected to the electricity grid. Whilst this is not the place to discuss the large number of energy efficiency and DSM options which can be readily implemented, (see, for example, Eberhard & van Horen 1995: 174-182), it is important that policy interventions dealing with externalities are part of an integrated approach which balances cost pressures on the supply side with potential gains on the demand side.

## The role of electricity prices in industrial policy

Electricity prices play an important role in a resource-intensive economy such as South Africa's. Equally, any increase in prices which may come about as a result of shifting the burden of environmental costs from society at large, to electricity producers and consumers, could have significant economic effects. At a microeconomic level, the price elasticity of demand (responsiveness to price changes) is relatively low in the short term, for the main reason that it is usually not easy to switch from electricity to an alternative energy source, particularly for large consumers. In the longer term, however, prices may play a larger role at the microeconomic level. This effect probably depends largely on the nature of the consumer, since electricity is a small input cost for most commercial, industrial and high-income domestic consumers and so they are more likely to absorb (and, where relevant, pass on) price increases. For large consumers, however, even small price changes can have a major effect on their competitiveness – for example, gold mines and aluminium producers.

At a macroeconomic level, electricity prices have an important effect on GDP, inflation and employment, since electricity is an intermediate good which affects most sectors of the economy. In the short term, any price increases can be expected to have a negative effect on these variables; this was confirmed by a macroeconomic modelling exercise undertaken by Gibson and van Seventer

(1995). In the longer term, however, it is less clear what the effects of higher electricity prices are on macroeconomic performance. Two of the most successful economies in the world, those of Japan and Germany, were built up from almost nothing after World War II, with energy prices which are amongst the highest in the world. This is not to suggest that their successful economic performance was a result simply of high energy prices – clearly it was not – and it is also not to suggest that a similar approach would necessarily succeed in South Africa fifty years later.

A highly pertinent question is whether cheap energy prices will be in South Africa's best interests in the long term, or whether they may lock the country into a resource-intensive development path as opposed to a higher value-added route. Or is there a middle route in which both of these sectors can be supported? It is beyond the scope of this study to suggest any answers to these questions, but it is important that they be posed and considered.

## Conclusion

This study has provided a range of estimates of the external costs of coal and nuclear electricity generation in South Africa. The results suggest that these costs, which were calculated, for the most part, with reference to direct costs arising in the economy, are significant in relation to current electricity prices. At the same time, there is an unavoidable degree of uncertainty over some of these estimates, as well as an understatement due to the omission of externalities for which insufficient data exists. From a policy perspective, the assessment of external costs constitutes an important building block in planning and investment decisions, and should be accounted for in a systematic manner across all sectors.

# Appendix 1
## Technical and geographic data on power stations

| | Province | Latitude (degrees S) | Longitude (degrees E) | Altitude | Units produced (GW) | Net capacity (MW) |
|---|---|---|---|---|---|---|
| Arnot* | Mpumalanga | 25.9500 | 29.8000 | 1 700 m | 4 557.5 | 1 955 |
| Duvha | Mpumalanga | 25.9667 | 29.333 | 1 596 m | 21 970.0 | 3 450 |
| Hendrina | Mpumalanga | 26.0333 | 29.6000 | 1 000 m | 11 871.2 | 1 900 |
| Kendal | Mpumalanga | 26.1000 | 28.9667 | 1 610 m | 19 396.8 | 3 840 |
| Kriel | Mpumalanga | 26.2500 | 29.1833 | 1 619 m | 13 394.5 | 2 850 |
| Lethabo | Free State | 26.7333 | 27.9667 | 1 460 m | 17 863.1 | 3 558 |
| Matimba | N. Prov. | 23.6667 | 27.6167 | 880 m | 22 685.2 | 3 690 |
| Matla | Mpumalanga | 26.2833 | 29.1333 | 1 620 m | 18 737.2 | 3 450 |
| Tutuka | Mpumalanga | 26.7667 | 29.3500 | 1 625 m | 17 522.9 | 3 510 |

\* Only two of Arnot's six sets were in operation in 1994.

**Table A1**   Eskom's coal power stations: location, output and capacity, 1994

| | Stack height (m) | Internal diameter (m) | Aggregated diameter (m) | Ave flue gas velocities (m/s) | Flue gas temp (degrees C) |
|---|---|---|---|---|---|
| Arnot | 193 | 8.00 | 11.31 | 4.0 | 138 |
| Duvha | 300 | 7.13 | 10.08 | 21.0 | 141 |
| Hendrina | 110 | 13.00 | 18.38 | 8.5 | 128 |
| Kendal | 275 | 7.46 | 10.55 | 21.0 | 127 |
| Kriel | 213 | 13.82 | 19.55 | 11.2 | 110 |
| Lethabo | 275 | 7.46 | 10.55 | 23.5 | 135 |
| Matimba | 250 | 7.52 | 10.63 | 19.5 | 130 |
| Matla | 278 & 213 | 6.32 | 8.94 | 9.3 | 130 |
| Tutuka | 275 | 6.45 | 9.12 | 31.0 | 135 |

\* Aggregated diameter for two chimneys calculated by multiplying single diameter by square root of 2.

\*\* Averaged, where necessary.

**Table A2**   Eskom's coal power stations:
stack dimensions and flue gas data

# Appendix 2
## Cost of illness data

| | Pneumonia | | | Asthma | | | COPD | | |
|---|---|---|---|---|---|---|---|---|---|
| | *mild* | *mod.* | *sev.* | *mild* | *mod.* | *sev.* | *mild* | *mod.* | *sev.* |
| % of cases[1] | 70 | 25 | 5 | 70 | 25 | 5 | 70 | 25 | 5 |
| Outpatient visits per case p.a. | 0.5 | 0.5 | 0.5 | 2 | 6 | 12 | 2 | 6 | 12 |
| GP visits per case p.a. | 0.5 | 0.5 | 0.5 | 2 | 6 | 12 | 2 | 6 | 12 |
| Days in general ward per case | 0 | 12 | 8 | 0 | 0 | 5 | 0 | 0 | 5 |
| Days in ICU per case (R) | 0 | 0 | 7 | 0 | 0 | 1 | 0 | 0 | 1 |
| Drug costs p.a. (R)[2] | incl. | incl. | incl. | 180 | 720 | 1 440 | 180 | 720 | 1440 |
| Cost per outpatient visit (R) | 30 | — | — | 30 | 60 | 90 | 30 | 60 | 90 |
| Cost per GP visit (R) | 100 | 100 | 100 | 100 | 100 | 100 | 100 | 100 | 100 |
| Cost per general ward day(R)[3] | — | 200 | 200 | — | — | 200 | — | — | 200 |
| Cost per ICU day (R)[4] | — | — | 1 616 | — | — | 1 616 | — | — | 1 616 |
| Transport costs per case (R)[5] | 10 | 130 | 320 | 40 | 120 | 360 | 40 | 120 | 360 |
| Persondays work missed per case (R)[6] | 1 | 13 | 16 | 4 | 12 | 30 | 4 | 12 | 30 |
| Cost per workday missed (R)[7] | 126 | 126 | 126 | 126 | 126 | 126 | 126 | 126 | 126 |
| Total (R) | 201 | 4233 | 15313 | 1104 | 3792 | 15228 | 1104 | 3792 | 15228 |

See notes for this table on next page

**Table B1**  Cost of illness data for pneumonia, asthma and chronic obstructive pulmonary disease

**Notes to Table B1**

1. Most of this data is based on discussions with Drs George Swingler and Anne Robertson, Red Cross Hospital, Cape Town, and Dr Rodney Ehrlich, Department of Community Health, UCT.

2. Based on estimated cost per inhaler of R100 for private care and R50 for public care, and a split of 20:80 for private:public care, giving a weighted average of R60 per inhaler. Mild cases will use 4 per annum, moderate will use 12 per annum and severe cases 24 per annum.

3. Based on analysis of hospital costs in former Cape Province, supplied by Dale McMurchy, Health Economics Unit, UCT.

4. Based on standard rates for general ICU according to Cape Medical Plan. Specialised ICU rates are R3034 per day, but these have not been used in this study.

5. Transport costs assumed to be R10 per person per return visit to the hospital, clinic or GP. For cases of patients admitted to hospital, it is assumed that there will be one visitor per admission day.

6. In the case of ICU admissions, it is assumed that one care-giver will miss work for each day the patient is in hospital.

7. Based on 1993 average wage in non-agricultural sector of R2 527 per month (South African Statistics 1994: 4.14) and a 22 day working month; inflated by 10% to give 1994 daily wage of R126.

# Summary of cost estimates

1. Respiratory hospital admissions (RHA, for pneumonia, asthma, COPD): weighted average cost per admission = (25/30 x R4233) + (5/30 x R15313) = R6080 per admission for pneumonia, and for asthma and COPD = (25/30 x R3792) + (5/30 x R15228) = R5698 per admission. Assume each accounts for a third of RHA, then weighted average cost of RHA is R5825 per admission.

2. Emergency room visits (outpatients) for pneumonia: average cost per visit = R201.

3. Asthma attacks (mild): average cost per occurrence-day = R1104/4 = R276.

4. Persons with mild COPD (e.g. chronic bronchitis): estimated cost per year = R1104.

5. Lifetime cost of mild COPD = R1104 pa at a real discount rate of 2% over 40 years = R30200, rounded down to R30000.

# References

African National Congress (ANC) 1994. *The reconstruction and development programme: a planning framework.* Umanyamo Publications. Johannesburg.

Annegarn, H 1995. *Air quality.* Draft report. Environmental Sciences Association. Johannesburg.

Auf der Heyde, T 1993. *The South African nuclear industry: history and prospects.* Energy for Development Research Centre. University of Cape Town.

Bernow, S, Becker, M, Biewald, B, Gurney, K, Loh, P, Shapiro, K & Wulfsberg, K 1991. *Valuation of environmental externalities for electric utility resource planning in Wisconsin.* Tellus Institute. Boston.

Bernow, S, Rowe, R, White, D, Bailly, K & Goldstein, J 1995a. *New York state environmental externalities cost study, report 3: user and reference manual.* Tellus Institute and RCG/Hagler, Bailly, Inc., Empire State Electric Energy Research Corporation. Albany.

Bernow, S, Rowe, R, White, D, Bailly, K & Goldstein, J 1995b. *New York state environmental externalities cost study, report 4: case studies.* Tellus Institute and RCG/Hagler, Bailly, Inc. Empire State Electric Energy Research Corporation. Albany.

Baumol, W J & Oates, W E 1988. *The theory of environmental policy.* Cambridge University Press. Second edition. Cambridge.

Carnevali, D & Suarez, C 1993. Electricity and the environment: air pollutant emissions in Argentina. *Energy Policy.* Vol. 21. No. 1.

Central Statistical Services (CSS) 1994. *South African labour statistics 1994.* CSS. Pretoria.

Clarke, J 1991. The insane experiment: tampering with the atmosphere. In Cock, J & Koch, E (Eds.), *Going green: people politics and the environment in South Africa.* Oxford University Press. Cape Town.

Cline, W R 1992 *The economics of global warming.* Institute for International Economics. Washington.

Coase, R H 1960. The problem of social cost. *Journal of law and economics.* No. 3.

Coetzee, H & Cooper, D 1991. Wasting water: squandering a precious resource. In Cock, J & Koch, E (Eds.), *Going green: people politics and the environment in South Africa.* Oxford University Press. Cape Town.

Cooper, C 1981. *Economic evaluation and the environment: a methodological discussion with particular reference to developing countries.* Hodder and Stoughton. London.

Department of Mineral and Energy Affairs (DMEA) 1995. *South African energy policy discussion document.* DMEA. Pretoria.

Department of Water Affairs and Forestry (DWAF) 1995. *Bulk water tariffs in South Africa: a possible new approach?* Paper presented at a conference on Water Conservation. Department of Water Affairs and Forestry. Pretoria.

De Villiers, M G & Dutkiewicz, R K 1993. The Cape Town brown haze study. Conference of National Association for Clean Air. Brits.

Diekmann, U & Notten, P 1995. Life cycle assessment: a tool for technology choices in the South African coal industry. Department of Chemical Engineering. University of Cape Town.

Dingley, C 1992. Institutional frameworks for the electricity supply industry. In Theron, P (ed.). *Proceedings of the ANC national meeting on electrification.* ANC Department of Economic Planning. Centre for Development Studies. Cape Town.

Du Plooy, D 1995. Personal communication. Fuels and water manager. Eskom. Johannesburg.

Dutkiewicz, R K & de Villiers, M G 1993. *Social cost of electricity production.* Engineering Research. Report for the National Energy Council. Pretoria.

Eberhard, A & van Horen, C 1995. *Poverty and power: Energy and the South African state.* UCT Press and Pluto Press. Cape Town and London.

Environmental Monitoring Group (EMG) & African National Congress (ANC) 1994. *Proceedings of the Conference on nuclear policy for a democratic South Africa.* Cape Town. 11-13 February.

Eskom 1992. *Annual report 1991.* Eskom. Johannesburg.

Eskom 1994. *Eskom statistical yearbook 1993.* Eskom . Johannesburg.

Eskom 1995a. *Annual report 1994.* Eskom. Johannesburg.

Eskom 1995b. *Eskom environmental report 1994.* Eskom. Johannesburg.

ETSU 1995. *Externalities of fuel cycles: "ExternE" project Summary report.* Report number 1. Prepared for the Commission of European Communities. Harwell. UK.

Fankhauser, S 1992. *Global warming damage costs: some monetary estimates.* Working paper GEC 92-29. Centre for Social and Economic Research on the Global Environment (CSERGE). London.

Fankhauser, S 1995. *Valuing climate change: the economics of the greenhouse.* Earthscan. London.

Fedorsky, C 1995. Personal communication. Generation Environment Manager. Eskom. Johannesburg.

Fisher, A C 1981. *Resource and environmental economics.* Cambridge University Press. Cambridge.

Fraser, M 1995. Personal communication. Water management section. Eskom. Johannesburg.

Freeman, A M 1993. *The measurement of environmental and resource values: theory and methods.* Resources for the Future. Washington.

Friedrich, R & Voss, A 1993. External costs of electricity generation. *Energy Policy.* Vol. 21. No. 2.

Gibson, B & van Seventer, D E 1995. The macroeconomic and environmental implications of green trade restrictions on South Africa. Draft paper. July 1995.

Government Mining Engineer (GME) 1995. Accident report from 01Jan94 to 31Dec95. Pretoria.

Hanson, R 1992. Personal communication. Generation group. Eskom. Johannesburg.

Helm, D & Pearce, D 1990. The assessment: economic policy towards the environment. *Oxford Review of Economic Policy*. Vol. 6. No. 1.

Hohmeyer, O 1988. *Social costs of energy consumption*. Springer Verlag. Berlin.

Hohmeyer, O & Gartner, M 1992. *The costs of climate change*. Fraunhofer Institut fur Systemtechnik und Innovationsforschung.

Jacobs, M 1991. *The green economy: environment, sustainable development and the politics of the future*. Pluto Press. London.

King, H A & Rodseth, K L 1993. *Gaseous detoxification technologies*. TRR/P93/083. Eskom TRI. Johannesburg.

Krupnick, A J, Markandya, A & Nickell, E 1993. The external costs of nuclear power: ex ante damages and lay risks. *American journal of agricultural economics*. Vol 75, December.

Lee, R 1995. Externalities studies: why are the numbers different? Paper presented at the Third International Workshop on Externality Costs. Ladenburg. Germany. 27-30 May 1995.

Lennon, S J & Turner C R 1992. Air quality impacts in South Africa: addressing common misconceptions. *Journal of Energy Research and Development in Southern Africa*. May.

Leon Commission 1995. *Commission of inquiry into safety and health in the mining industry*. Department of Mineral and Energy Affairs. Pretoria.

Lerer, L 1995. Review of the bio-medical literature relating to energy and health. Medical Research Council. Cape Town.

Levy, M A 1995. International co-operation to combat acid rain. In Bergesen, H E & Parmann, G (Eds.), *Green globe yearbook of international co-operation on environment and development*. Oxford University Press. Oxford.

Lockwood, B 1992. *The social costs of electricity generation*. Report GEC 92-09. Centre for Social and Economic Research on the Global Environment (CSERGE). University of East Anglia and University College London.

MacKerron, G 1992. Nuclear costs: why do they keep rising? *Energy Policy*. Vol. 20, No. 7.

Meyer, A & Cooper, T 1995. A recalculation of the social costs of climate change. Global Commons Institute. London.

Minerals Bureau 1994. *South Africa's mineral industry: 1993/94*. Department of Minerals and Energy Affairs. Pretoria.

Nordhaus, W D 1993. Reflections on the economics of climate change policy. *Journal of economic perspectives*. Vol. 7, No. 4.

Oak Ridge National Laboratory (ORNL) and Resources for the Future (RFF) 1994a. *Estimating fuel cycle externalities: analytical methods and issues*. Report No. 2. McGraw-Hill/ Utility Data Institute. Washington.

Oak Ridge National Laboratory (ORNL) and Resources for the Future (RFF) 1994b. *Estimating externalities of coal fuel cycles*. Report No. 3. McGraw-Hill/ Utility Data Institute. Washington.

Oak Ridge National Laboratory (ORNL) and Resources for the Future (RFF) 1995a. *Estimating externalities of natural gas fuel cycles.* Report No. 4. McGraw-Hill/ Utility Data Institute. Washington.

Oak Ridge National Laboratory (ORNL) and Resources for the Future (RFF) 1995b. *Estimating externalities of oil fuel cycles.* Report No. 5. McGraw-Hill/ Utility Data Institute. Washington.

Oak Ridge National Laboratory (ORNL) and Resources for the Future (RFF) 1995c. *Estimating externalities of hydro fuel cycles.* Report No. 6. McGraw-Hill/ Utility Data Institute. Washington.

Oak Ridge National Laboratory (ORNL) and Resources for the Future (RFF) 1995d. *Estimating externalities of biomass fuel cycles.* Report No. 7. McGraw-Hill/ Utility Data Institute. Washington.

Oak Ridge National Laboratory (ORNL) and Resources for the Future (RFF) 1995e. *Estimating externalities of nuclear fuel cycles.* Report No. 8. McGraw-Hill/ Utility Data Institute. Washington.

Olbrich, K A & Kruger, F J 1990. Indications of air pollution effects on Pinus Patula in the Eastern & Southern Transvaal. 1st IUAPPA Regional conference. Pretoria.

Olbrich, K, van Tienhoven, M, Skoroszewski, R, Zunckel, M & Taljaard, J 1995. *A prototype atmospheric risk advisory system for the Eastern Transvaal province.* Draft report FOR-I 547. Council for Scientific and Industrial Research. Pretoria.

Ottinger, R L 1995. Have recent externality studies rendered environmental externality valuation irrelevant? Paper presented at the Third International Workshop on Externality Costs. Ladenburg. Germany. 27-30 May 1995.

Ottinger, R L, Wooley, D R, Robinson, N A, Hodas, D R & Babb, S 1991. *Environmental costs of electricity.* Oceana Publications Inc. New York.

Palmer Development Group (PDG) 1995. *The potential market for low-smoke coal.* Draft report for the Department of Mineral and Energy Affairs. Pretoria.

Pearce, D W 1995. The development of externality adders in the United Kingdom. Workshop on: the External Costs of Energy. Brussels. 30-31 January 1995.

Pearce, D, Markandya, A & Barbier, E 1989. *Blueprint for a green economy.* Earthscan. London.

Pearce, D W & Turner, R K 1990. *Economics of natural resources and the environment.* Harvester Wheatsheaf. Hemel Hempstead. UK.

Pearce, D, Barbier, E, Markandya, A, Barrett, S, Turner, R K & Swanson, T 1991. *Blueprint 2: greening the world economy.* Earthscan. London.

Pearce, D W, Bann, C & Georgiou, S 1992. *The social costs of fuel cycles.* HMSO. London.

Piketh, S J & Annegarn, H J 1994. Dry deposition of sulphate aerosols and acid rain potential in the Eastern Transvaal and Lowveld regions. National Association for Clean Air Conference. Cape Town.

Pigou, A C 1920. *The economics of welfare.* Macmillan. London.

Raimondo, J, van Zyl, H, Bonner, D & Brownlie, S 1995. *Environmental cost internalisation in the South African coal mining industry.* Draft report for UNCTAD, Cape Town.

Roome, J 1995. Water pricing and management. World Bank. Presentation at a conference on Water Conservation. Department of Water Affairs and Forestry. Pretoria.

Roos, G 1995. Personal communications. Eskom TRI. Johannesburg.

Rorich, R P & Turner, C R 1994. *Ambient monitoring network:: annual data report for 1993 and regional long-term trend analysis.* Report no. TRR/S94/059/rw. Eskom TRI. Johannesburg.

Rowe, R, Lang, C, Bird, L, Callaway, M, Chestnut, L, Eldridge, M, Latimer, D, Lipton, J & Rae, D 1994. *New York state environmental externalities cost study, report 1: externalities screening and recommendations.* RCG/Hagler, Bailly, Inc. Empire State Electric Energy Research Corporation. Albany.

Rowe, R D, Bernow, S S, Bird, L A, Callaway, J M, Chestnut, L G, Eldridge, M M, Lang, C M, Latimer, D A, Murdoch, J C, Ostro, B D, Patterson, A K, Rae, D A, White, D E 1994. *New York state environmental externalities cost study, report 2: methodology.* RCG/Hagler, Bailly, Inc. Empire State Electric Energy Research Corporation. Albany.

Rowe, R D, Chestnut, L G, Lang, C M, Bernow, S S & White, D E 1995. The New York environmental externalities cost study: summary of approach and results. Workshop on: the External Costs of Energy. Brussels. 30-31 January 1995.

Rowlands, I R 1995a. *The climate change negotiations: Berlin and beyond.* Discussion paper 17. Centre for the Study of Global Governance. London School of Economics.

Rowlands, I R 1995b. South Africa and global climate change. Draft paper. London School of Economics.

Schleisner, L, Meyer, H J & Mothorst, P E 1995. Assessment of environmental external effects in the production of energy. Workshop on: the External Costs of Energy. Brussels. 30-31 January 1995.

Scholes, R J 1995. Personal communication. CSIR Forestek. Pretoria.

Stavins, R N 1995. Transaction costs and markets for pollution control. *Resources.* Resources for the Future. No. 119.

Steyn, G 1994. *Restructuring the South African electricity supply industry.* Paper 14a. Energy Policy Research and Training Project. Energy for Development Research Centre. University of Cape Town.

Terblanche, P 1995. Personal communication. CSIR Environmental Services. Pretoria.

Terblanche, P, Nel, C M E & Opperman, L 1992. *Health and safety aspects of domestic fuels.* Report to the National Energy Council. Medical Research Council. Pretoria.

Terblanche, P, Nel, C M E & Opperman, L 1993. *Health and safety aspects of domestic fuels: phase 2.* Report to the Department of Mineral and Energy Affairs. Pretoria.

Tilley, H A & Keir, J 1994. *1993 KED database.* Report no. TRR/P94/127. Eskom TRI. Johannesburg.

Turner, C R 1987. An assessment of air pollution in the Eastern Transvaal Highveld. Air Pollution Conference 'Two Decades of Progress?'. CSIR. Pretoria.

Turner, C R 1993. A seven year study of rainfall chemistry in South Africa. National Association for Clean Air conference. 11-12 November, Brits.

Turner, C R 1994a. *Visibility impairment in the rural Eastern Transvaal Highveld region.* Report no. TRR/S94/164/rw. Eskom TRI. Johannesburg.

Turner, C R 1994b. *Deposition studies: progress report for 1994.* Report no. TRR/S94/207/rw. Eskom TRI. Johannesburg.

Turner, C R 1995. Personal communications. Eskom TRI. Johannesburg.

Turner, C R, Tosen, G R, Lennon, S J & Blackbeard, P J 1990. Eskom's Air Quality Impacts - a regional perspective. World Energy Council Forum. Harare.

Tyson, P D, Kruger, F J & Louw, C W 1988. *Atmospheric pollution and its implications in the Eastern Transvaal Highveld.* South African National Scientific Programmes. Report no 150. Pretoria.

Van Horen, C 1994. *Household energy and environment.* Paper 16. South African Energy Policy Research and Training Project. Energy for Development Research Centre. University of Cape Town.

Van Horen, C 1995. Eskom, its finances and the national electrification programme. *Development Southern Africa.* October. In press.

Van Horen, C & Simmonds, G 1995. Greenhouse gas abatement in South Africa's energy sector. Paper presented at the Regional Workshop on greenhouse gas mitigation for African countries. Arusha, Tanzania. 28 - 30 August 1995.

Van Pletsen, J L 1994. Investment opportunities offered by electricity. *World economic development congress.* New York. 2-3 June 1994.

Van Rensburg, D T J 1994. *Environmental contributions to atmospheric corrosion (3rd year).* Report no. TRR/S94/194/djvr. Eskom TRI. Johannesburg.

Von Schirnding, Y E R, Yach, D & Klein, M 1991. Acute respiratory infections as an important cause of childhood deaths in South Africa. *South African Medical Journal.* Vol. 80, No. 2.

Weather Bureau 1975. *Climate of South Africa: part 12 surface winds.* Weather Bureau. Pretoria.

Wells, B 1993. *Acidic dry deposition on the Highveld.* CSIR internal report. EMAP-I 93004. Pretoria.

World Bank 1993. *World development report 1992.* Oxford University Press. Oxford.